RONALD REAGAN

Quotes & Quips

RONALD
REAGAN

Quotes & Quips

★ ★ ★

EDITED BY David Stanford Burr

Brimming with creative inspiration, how-to projects, and useful information to enrich your everyday life, Quarto Knows is a favorite destination for those pursuing their interests and passions. Visit our site and dig deeper with our books into your area of interest: Quarto Creates, Quarto Cooks, Quarto Homes, Quarto Lives, Quarto Drives, Quarto Explores, Quarto Gifts, or Quarto Kids.

This edition published in 2018 by Crestline, an imprint of The Quarto Group, 142 West 36th Street, 4th Floor, New York, NY 10018, USA
T (212) 779-4972 **F** (212) 779-6058
www.QuartoKnows.com

First published in the United States of America in 2015 by Wellfleet Press, an imprint of The Quarto Group, 142 West 36th Street, 4th Floor, New York, NY 10018, USA

Crestline titles are also available at discount for retail, wholesale, promotional, and bulk purchase. For details, contact the Special Sales Manager by email at specialsales@quarto.com or by mail at The Quarto Group, Attn: Special Sales Manager, 401 Second Avenue North, Suite 310, Minneapolis, MN 55401, USA.

Ronald Reagan's baby portrait, 1911, page 6, courtesy of the Ronald Reagan Presidential Foundation. All other photos courtesy of the Ronald Reagan Library.

10 9 8 7 6 5 4 3 2 1

ISBN: 978-0-7858-3662-9

Printed in China

CONTENTS

President Reagan at a rally for Senator David Durenberger in Minneapolis, Minnesota, January 8, 1982.

Introduction

A STRONG RELIGIOUS GROUNDING, A SOLID MORAL character, and a compelling ability to communicate his personal vision, often with humor, fostered the larger-than-life personality of Ronald Reagan, fortieth President of the United States.

The bedrock of Ronald Reagan's early religious upbringing was his mother Nelle's devout adherence to the Disciples of Christ—a Christian Protestant denomination that lobbied for Prohibition—and her unshakable faith in human goodness and that God had a reason for whatever happened. Nelle's husband, Jack, a nominal Irish Catholic and on-again-off-again alcoholic salesman proved a trial to the family but Nelle insisted that her sons adopt the advanced view that his was a disease and not a moral failure. "Dutch" Reagan was baptized into the Disciples, attended and worked in the church, acted in church plays, and matriculated at the Disciples-based Eureka College, where he thrived. Ronald Reagan became a Presbyterian as an adult, but maintained a lifelong belief in his boyhood precepts and was confident that adversity was a test of character and that God had a plan for him—that he had a rendezvous with destiny.

Much of Reagan's moral character was founded on his religious and family rearing, and he embodied an ambitious work ethic that led to successful careers in radio and television. His good nature, integrity, decency, and optimism propelled him forward. Reagan displayed courage by bucking the trend to follow his ideals and abandoned his early Roosevelt liberal democrat convictions for conservative principles that would take him decades later to the leadership of the Republican Party. At one point the president of a Hollywood union, he would later as President break a union-led air traffic controllers' strike. His passionate vision in advocating for lessened government interference in citizens' lives, free market trade, reduced taxes, and taking a hard line on rolling back communism were made all the more compelling because of his presidential and statesman demeanor and a contagious optimism for a better future for the United States and the world.

Reagan gave his first speech as part of a student strike at Eureka College and he realized that mass media might be in his stars. As radio announcer, Hollywood actor (and one of its union leaders), television personality, and spokesman for General Electric— writing and delivering many public speeches—Reagan benefitted from a profound and unique apprenticeship that evolved during his years as Governor and President, and he was popularly acknowledged as the Great Communicator. A quick study with a natural, genial manner and masterful timing and delivery he put his audience at ease, making them more receptive to his message. He was a natural storyteller, like his father, and often alluded to values of patriotism, freedom, and progress and to God's authority. He consoled the country after the *Challenger* disaster, exhorted Gorbachev to tear down the Berlin Wall dividing Germany, poignantly

Formal photograph of Ronald Reagan, 1934.

Ronald Reagan at Rancho del Cielo, 1976.

eulogized the fallen at the Fortieth Anniversary of the Normandy Invasion, and steered the ship of state through eight years of calm and storm with his hand steady on the tiller and with a voice resolute to engage and encourage the American dream.

Central to Reagan's oratory was his ability to broadly elicit goodwill and deflect criticism through humor. The oldest President to take the oath of office at sixty-nine, then a second term at seventy-three, he—as well as his detractors—was aware of his age and often poked fun at himself on the issue. Many learned to their disadvantage that he was not the simple man he projected as he self-assuredly and good-naturedly skewered his opponents with one-liners and witticisms leaving them confused and frustrated. With an arsenal of anecdotes and an easy banter he was the nation's salesman-in-chief and his humor and bonhomie helped him sail through the few rough times of his presidency relatively unassailed—reflected in another popular Reagan moniker, the Teflon president.

This offering of *Ronald Reagan: Quotes & Quips* relies on the man, the citizen, and the President in his own words, presented within a ten-chapter biographical framework. Interspersed among the quotations and their attributions are Did You Know? trivia segments providing interesting tidbits of information about Reagan, along with longer, boxed excerpts titled "The Storyteller" and "The Great Communicator." Also, consult the index for Reagan topic headings.

Ronald Reagan's baby portrait, 1911.

1

A Rendezvous with Destiny

You know an awful lot more about being young than you
do about being old.

> —from Q&A with the students and faculty at
> Moscow State University, May 31, 1988

RONALD WILSON REAGAN WAS BORN ON FEBRUARY 6, 1911, IN
Tampico, a small town in Illinois, to Jack, a great storyteller
and an unsuccessful salesman with a drinking problem,
and Nelle, an active churchgoer and frustrated actress. The Reagan
family—brother John Neil (called "Moon" after the popular comic
strip character Moon Mullins) was born in 1908—moved around
quite a lot and came to settle in Dixon, Illinois, in 1920. Young
Ronald, or "Dutch" as his father nicknamed him at birth, took a
keen interest in sports, especially football and swimming, but it was
not until he was diagnosed at age thirteen with nearsightedness
that he realized why he was not so good at baseball. He was

outgoing and popular but only an average student, whose talent for memorization often saved him from bad grades.

Due to his swimming skill, he became a lifeguard at the nearby Rock River in his second year in high school, a job he held for seven summers, during which he saved seventy-seven people from drowning. Not a stellar football player, Dutch did get a partial football scholarship to the small Eureka College, near Peoria, working several jobs during the school term and summers to stay in school. He was a starting guard on the football team, and varsity captain of the swim team, and ran relays for the track team. He continued his high school interest in dramatics, and in his senior year was elected class president. He made good grades and graduated in 1932 with a B.A. in economics and sociology.

According to family legend, when my father ran up the stairs and looked at his newborn son, he quipped: "He looks like a fat little Dutchman. But who knows, he might grow up to be president some day."

—from *An American Life: The Autobiography*
by Ronald Reagan

I can remember one bleak night in the thirties when my father learned on Christmas Eve that he'd lost his job. To be young in my generation was to feel that your future had been mortgaged out from under you, and that's a tragic mistake we must never allow our leaders to make again. Today's young people must never be held hostage to the mistakes of the past. The only way to avoid making those mistakes again is to learn from them.

—from Address to the Nation,
October 13, 1982

Did You Know? ★ When Dutch was eleven he came home one night and found his father passed out on the porch. It was snowing and cold and the boy just wanted to go to bed and leave his father there, but he dragged him into the house and got him to bed. Jack had periods of sobriety, but they would always be short-lived. In 1941, Jack finally swore to Nelle that he would give up liquor and poured a bottle down the drain. Sadly, John Edward "Jack" Reagan died two weeks later of a heart attack at age fifty-eight.

America was founded by people who believed that God was their rock of safety. He is ours. I recognize we must be cautious in claiming that God is on our side, but I think it's all right to keep asking if we're on His side.

—from State of the Union Address,
January 25, 1984

I learned from my father the value of hard work and ambition, and maybe a little something about telling a story.

From my mother, I learned the value of prayer, how to have dreams and believe I could make them come true.

—from *An American Life*

Mothers are the creators of the family, and the family is the center of society. It's no accident that America chose to honor all mothers with a special holiday. After all, mothers have made a unique contribution to our country. They're the main communicators of the values by which our nation has flourished for more than two hundred years—the values of honesty, responsibility, decency, and personal effort. By imparting these and other values to our children, the mothers of America quite literally shape the future.

—from Radio Address to the Nation on Mother's Day, May 11, 1985

Did You Know? ★ Nelle Wilson Reagan and her husband, Jack, moved out to Hollywood, California, into a house Ronald bought for them. Nelle was widowed in 1941, and she later developed senility, now called Alzheimer's disease. She died from complications of the disease when she was seventy-nine in 1962. Ronald at age eighty-three was diagnosed with Alzheimer's and would die ten years later.

T H E   S T O R Y T E L L E R

I noticed that I told you about one of my first jobs as a young man, working for a contractor who was remodeling old homes. I was just fourteen years old—by the way, it's not true that the homes that we were remodeling were log cabins. As I say, I was just fourteen years old; and as I told you, by the time the summer was over, I'd dug out foundations, laid hardwood floors, shingled roofs, and learned a respect for good, honest labor that has stayed with me all my life. But my notes show that I never did tell you just how it was that I left that construction work.

Well, it was on that summer job—this time digging trenches for foundations. And one hot morning I was swinging my pickax, working away, swinging and digging. It so happened that I had the pick up over my head, ready to bring it down in another blow, when the noon whistle blew. And I just stepped out from under the pickax and didn't finish the blow—it was after twelve o'clock—and walked out from under it. And right behind me, I heard some words that my mother had told me never to use. I turned around, and there was my boss, standing there, with the point of the pick stuck in the ground right between his feet—I missed him by about a half an inch. And although I can't say for certain, looking back, but I have the feeling that it may have been at that moment, looking into his face, that I first entertained the thoughts of going into show business.

—FROM WHITE HOUSE MEETING WITH THE ASSOCIATED GENERAL
CONTRACTORS OF AMERICA, APRIL 18, 1988

No one who lived through the Great Depression can ever look upon an unemployed person with anything but compassion. To me, there is no greater tragedy than a breadwinner willing to work, with a job skill but unable to find a market for that job skill. Back in those dark Depression days I saw my father on Christmas Eve open what he thought was a Christmas greeting from his boss. Instead, it was the blue slip telling him he no longer had a job. The memory of him sitting there holding that slip of paper and then saying in a half whisper, "That's quite a Christmas present"; it will stay with me as long as I live.

—from "To Restore America"
(Reagan's Campaign Address),
March 31, 1976

Well, one of the worst mistakes anybody can make is to bet against Americans.

—from Radio Address to the Nation,
May 16, 1987

Hard work never killed anyone, but I figure, why take the chance?
—from *Ronald Reagan: The Presidential Portfolio:
A History Illustrated from the Collection of the
Ronald Reagan Library and Museum* by Lou Cannon

THE STORYTELLER

Some years ago, when we were a young nation and our people began visiting the lands of their forefathers, these American tourists then were rather brash, unsophisticated by European standards, but blessed with a spirit of independence and pride. One such tourist, an elderly, small-town gentleman, and his wife were there in Europe listening to a tour guide go on about the wonders of the volcano, Mount Aetna. He spoke of the great heat that it generated, the power, the boiling lava, et cetera.

Finally the old boy had had enough of it, turned to his wife, and he said, "We've got a volunteer fire department at home that'd put that thing out in fifteen minutes." Well, he was typical of those Americans who helped build a neighbor's barn when it burned down. They built the West without an area redevelopment plan, and cities across the land without Federal planning.

—FROM ADDRESS TO THE NATION, SEPTEMBER 24, 1981

There are a thousand sparks of genius in fifty states and a thousand communities around the Nation. It is time to nurture them and see which ones can catch fire and become guiding lights.

—from State of the Union Address,
January 25, 1988

I . . . remember those Depression years. Times were tough. But what I remember most clearly is that Dixon held together.

Our faith was our strength. Our teachers pointed to the future. People held on to their hopes and dreams. Neighbors helped neighbors. We knew—my brother, Moon, and I, our mother and father, Nelle and Jack, saw to that—saw that we knew we would overcome adversity and that after the storm, the stars would come.
—from remarks during a homecoming and birthday celebration,
Dixon, Illinois, February 6, 1984

We hear much of special interest groups. Well, our concern must be for a special interest group that has been too long neglected. It knows no sectional boundaries or ethnic and racial divisions, and it crosses political party lines. It is made up of men and women who raise our food, patrol our streets, man our mines and factories, teach our children, keep our homes, and heal us when we're sick—professionals, industrialists, shopkeepers, clerks, cabbies, and truck drivers. They are, in short, "We the people," this breed called Americans.
—from First Presidential Inaugural Address,
January 20, 1981

Ronald Reagan (with "Dutch-boy" haircut), Neil Reagan, and parents, Jack and Nelle Reagan. Family Christmas card circa 1916–1917.

Ronald Reagan's fourth grade class photo in Tampico, Illinois, 1920 (Ronald Reagan is in the second row with his hand on his chin).

Ronald Reagan in Dixon, Illinois, 1920s.

Ronald Reagan on the Eureka College football team, 1929.

Loyalty, faithfulness, commitment, courage, patriotism, the ability to distinguish between right and wrong—I hope that these values are as much a part of your life as any calculus course or social science study.

—from presentation ceremony for the
Presidential Scholars Awards, June 16, 1988

Oh, you'll have some regrets along with the happy memories. I let football and other extracurricular activities eat into my study time with the result that my grade average was closer to the C level required for eligibility than it was to straight A's. And even now I wonder what I might have accomplished if I'd studied harder.

—from commencement exercises at Eureka College,
May 9, 1982

I loved playing on the line: For me, it was probably a marriage made in heaven. It's as fundamental as anything in life—a collision between two bodies, one determined to advance, the other determined to resist; one man against another man, blocking, tackling, breaking through the line.

—from *An American Life*

Did You Know? ★ Ronald Reagan was the first President to participate in a Super Bowl coin toss. For Super Bowl XIX (January 20, 1985), between the Miami Dolphins and the San Francisco 49ers, Reagan performed the coin toss via satellite from the White House. The 49ers won the game 38–16.

There's a lesson here that we all should write on the blackboard a hundred times: In a child's education, money can never take the place of basics like discipline, hard work, and, yes, homework.

—from State of the Union Address, January 25, 1988

Graduation Day is called "Commencement," and properly so, because it is both a recognition of completion and a beginning. And I would like, seriously, to talk to you about this new phase— the society in which you're now going to take your place as full-time participants. You're no longer observers. You'll be called upon to make decisions and express your views on global events, because those events will affect your lives.

—from commencement exercises at Eureka College, May 9, 1982

Twenty-five years after I graduated, my alma mater brought me back to the school and gave me an honorary degree. And I had to tell them they compounded a sense of guilt I had nursed for twenty-five years because I always felt the first degree they gave me was honorary.

—from Q&A with the students and faculty at Moscow State University, May 31, 1988

Ronald Reagan on a diving board, while on the Eureka College swim team, 1928–1932.

Yes, the deeds of infamy or injustice are all recorded, but what shines out from the pages of history is the daring of the dreamers and the deeds of the builders and the doers. These things make up the stories we tell and pass on to our children. They comprise the most enduring and striking fact about human history — that through the heartbreak and tragedy man has always dared to perceive the outline of human progress, the steady growth in not just the material well-being, but the spiritual insight of mankind.

— from 39th Session of the UN General Assembly, New York,

September 24, 1984

*Ronald Reagan as a radio announcer in
Des Moines, Iowa, 1934–1937.*

2

Radio Days and Hollywood Nights

You can't put a price tag on the American dream. That
dream is the heart and soul of America; it's the promise
that keeps our nation forever good and generous, a model
and hope to the world.

> —from signing the Tax Reform Act of 1986,
> October 22, 1986

AFTER GRADUATION, REAGAN SOUGHT EMPLOYMENT DURING
the Depression, when one of four Americans was
unemployed, which included his father. With no jobs in
Dixon, Reagan was determined to become a radio announcer and
got a tryout in Davenport, Iowa, announcing sports. He then moved
to Des Moines, Iowa, to announce Chicago Cubs baseball games
where he showed a knack at play-by-play descriptions that were only
sketchily provided by wire news services, and these re-creations
delivered with a warm, sincere, and resonant voice gained him
popularity in the Midwest, and he soon was sending money home.

In 1937, after a screen test in Los Angeles, Warner Brothers offered Reagan a seven-year contract and over the next five years he acted in nearly twenty B-movies, low-budget commercial endeavors, where he played wholesome and amiable characters — a bit of true-to-life typecasting — with such notable actors as Bette Davis, Humphrey Bogart, and Errol Flynn. In 1940 Reagan broke out of B-movies roles when he played George Gipp, the Notre Dame football star, in *Knute Rockne, All American*, where he delivered his famous line "Win just one for the Gipper." Reagan's role garnered critical praise. In 1942 he appeared in his favorite role in *Kings Row*, as a victim of a sadistic surgeon who amputates both Reagan's character's legs. When he comes out from under anesthesia, he utters the famous line, "Where's the rest of me?"

In 1941 Reagan was elected to the Board of Directors of the Screen Actors Guild (SAG) and after the Second World War served as vice president, then elected president (1947–1952, again in 1959). As his film career began to wane in the 1950s and with the popular rise of the television medium, Reagan switched careers and became the host of a weekly series, CBS's *General Electric Theater*. As a spokesman for GE he visited many GE plants where he wrote and delivered hundreds of nonpartisan but pro-business, anti-big-government, and anticommunist speeches with an amiable, self-deprecating style, a pivotal apprenticeship that would well serve his later political aspirations, when he would become known as "The Great Communicator."

He enjoyed a twenty-seven-year career in movies (making over fifty full-feature films) and either hosted or acted in hundreds of television shows.

Reagan won a Golden Globe Award (Hollywood Citizenship) in 1957 and a Golden Raspberry Award (Razzie) in 1981 for Worst Career Achievement.

★ ★ ★

Life is just one grand sweet song, so start the music.
—caption beneath Ronald Reagan's senior photograph in his high school yearbook, Dixon High School, 1928

Did You Know? ★ Reagan's film debut was *Love Is on the Air* (1937), where he played the role of a radio announcer.

One other thing we Americans like—the future—like the sound of it, the idea of it, the hope of it. Where others fear trade and economic growth, we see opportunities for creating new wealth and undreamed-of opportunities for millions in our own land and beyond. Where others seek to throw up barriers, we seek to bring them down. Where others take counsel of their fears, we follow our hopes. Yes, we Americans like the future and like making the most of it.

—from State of the Union Address, January 25, 1988

I took a train out to California and ended up with a movie contract at Warner Brothers. I was known as "Dutch" Reagan then, my childhood nickname. The studio didn't like it, so they called a meeting to discuss what my name should be. And I began to realize how expendable what you might call my identity was in this new business I was in. So, as they were throwing names back and forth, I was just sitting there listening. They acted as if I couldn't hear.

And finally, as they kept going on and trying out various names, looking up as if they were looking at a marquis, I timidly suggested one they hadn't thought of, my real name—Ronald Reagan. They started tossing it around the table. And I'll never forget the scene. The top man said it over and over to himself: "Ronald Reagan, Ronald Reagan." He paused for a long moment and then declared, "I like it." So, I became Ronald Reagan.

—from Franklin D. Roosevelt Library
50th Anniversary Luncheon, January 10, 1989

Remember, there are no limits to growth and human progress when men and women are free to follow their dreams. The American dream belongs to you; it lives in millions of different hearts; it can be fulfilled in millions of different ways.

—from Address to the Nation, May 28, 1985

Publicity photograph of Ronald Reagan, 1940s.

Still from the film **Knute Rockne, All American**, *1940.*

I've not taken your time this evening merely to ask you to trust me. Instead, I ask you to trust yourselves. That's what America is all about. Our struggle for nationhood, our unrelenting fight for freedom, our very existence—these have all rested on the assurance that you must be free to shape your life as you are best able to, that no one can stop you from reaching higher or take from you the creativity that has made America the envy of mankind.

—from Address to the Nation, July 27, 1981

Did You Know? ★ Reagan's famous line, "Win just one for the Gipper," was later used as his political campaign slogan, "Win one for the Gipper," and Reagan became widely known as "the Gipper."

Go for it! Reach those heights, excel, push yourself to the limits, strive for excellence. . . . You're free to be anything. You're free to be whatever you want to be with no one and nothing stopping you. In a free society, you're free to invent yourself—to turn yourself into a great teacher, a racecar driver, a minister, or a movie star, or a grower and seller of flowers. You can be anything. It's your invention. And there's nothing to stop you.

—from remarks at Northside High School,
Atlanta, Georgia, June 6, 1985

THE GREAT COMMUNICATOR

Go to any American town . . . and you'll see dozens of churches, representing many different beliefs—in many places, synagogues and mosques—and you'll see families of every conceivable nationality worshiping together. Go into any schoolroom, and there you will see children being taught the Declaration of Independence, that they are endowed by their Creator with certain unalienable rights—among them life, liberty, and the pursuit of happiness—that no government can justly deny; the guarantees in their Constitution for freedom of speech, freedom of assembly, and freedom of religion. Go into any courtroom, and there will preside an independent judge, beholden to no government power. There every defendant has the right to a trial by a jury of his peers, usually twelve men and women—common citizens; they are the ones, the only ones, who weigh the evidence and decide on guilt or innocence. In that court, the accused is innocent until proven guilty, and the word of a policeman or any official has no greater legal standing than the word of the accused. . . . March in any demonstration, and there are many of them; the people's right of assembly is guaranteed in the Constitution and protected by the police. Go into any union hall, where the members know their right to strike is protected by law. As a matter of fact, one of the many jobs I had before this one was being president of a union, the Screen Actors Guild. I led my union out on strike, and I'm proud to say we won.

—FROM Q&A WITH THE STUDENTS AND FACULTY AT
MOSCOW STATE UNIVERSITY, MAY 31, 1988

For years, I've heard the question: "How could an actor be president?" I've sometimes wondered how you could be president and not be an actor.

—from *An American Life*

Did You Know? ★ Reagan would reprise his famous line, "Where's the rest of me?" from *Kings Row*, as the title of his 1967 autobiography.

My message today is that the dreams of ordinary people reach to astonishing heights. If we diplomatic pilgrims are to achieve equal altitudes, we must build all we do on the full breadth of humanity's will and consent and the full expanse of the human heart.

—from 42nd Session of the UN General Assembly, New York, September 21, 1987

Before I took up my current line of work, I got to know a thing or two about negotiating when I represented the Screen Actors Guild in contract talks with the studios. After the studios, [Soviet General Secretary Mikhail] Gorbachev was a snap.

—from remarks to the National Chamber Foundation, November 17, 1988

I have to confess that I'm amazed that a Hollywood actor who costarred with a monkey could ever make it in politics.
— from White House Meeting with members of the American Business Conference, April 15, 1986, in regards to Clint Eastwood (who had become mayor of Carmel, California) starring alongside an orangutan in *Every Which Way but Loose* (1978) and *Any Which Way You Can* (1980)

Did You Know? ★ After a lull in his acting career in the late 1940s, Reagan starred in *Bedtime for Bonzo* (1951), a light comedy that also starred a chimpanzee named Bonzo. The movie became a box-office hit and for a while resurrected Reagan's acting career. Reagan later quipped that he had been asked to be in the sequel, *Bonzo Goes to College*, but in the Bonzo role.

[I]n Hollywood, when I was there, if you didn't sing or dance, you wound up as an after-dinner speaker. And I didn't sing or dance.
— from Q&A with the students and faculty at Moscow State University, May 31, 1988

You have a hell of an opening, coast for a while, and then you have a hell of a close.
— 1966 quip on how politics is like show business, *Ronald Reagan* by Michael Schaller

This [story has] to do with a fellow that applied to the zoo for a job. And they interviewed him and all and finally told him, yes, he could have the job. And when he came in in the morning, they said, "But I tell you, we lost our ape, and you'll have to take his place in this ape suit just until the next one arrives that we've sent for. And then you'll be at your regular job here in the zoo."

Well, he got into the suit, and they said, "You just get in the cage and just kind of move around. There's a rope in there you can swing on and stuff and entertain the children."

So, he did.

Well, he kind of got carried away with it after a while, with the children all looking at him and so forth. And finally he was swinging on that rope, and he swung too far—up over the top of the cage and dropped into the lion's cage. And the lion came roaring at him and jumped on him.

And he started screaming, "Get me out of here! Save me! Help me! Get me out of here!"

And the lion whispered, "Shut up, or you'll get us both fired!"

—FROM FUND-RAISING DINNER FOR
SENATOR DAVID K. KARNES OF NEBRASKA,
JULY 11, 1988

I've seen America from the stadium press box as a sportscaster, as an actor, officer of my labor union, soldier, officeholder, and as both Democrat and Republican. I've lived in an America where those who often had too little to eat outnumbered those who had enough. There have been four wars in my lifetime and I've seen our country face financial ruin in the Depression. I have also seen the great strength of this nation as it pulled itself up from that ruin to become the dominant force in the world.

To me our country is a living, breathing presence, unimpressed by what others say is impossible, proud of its own success, generous, yes, and naïve, sometimes wrong, never mean, and always impatient to provide a better life for its people in a framework of a basic fairness and freedom.

Someone once said that the difference between an American and any other kind of person is that an American lives in anticipation of the future because he knows it will be a great place. Other people fear the future as just a repetition of past failures. There's a lot of truth in that. If there is one thing we are sure of it is that history need not be relived; that nothing is impossible, and that man is capable of improving his circumstances beyond what we are told is fact.

—from announcement for 1980 presidential candidacy,
November 13, 1979

Ronald Reagan and General Electric Theater, *1954–1962.*

Engagement photo of Ronald Reagan and Nancy Davis, 1952.

3

Marriage and Fatherhood

Forty years ago, I entered a world of happiness. Nancy moved into my heart filling an empty spot with her love . . . From the start, our marriage was like an adolescent's dream of what a marriage should be. And for 40 years it has gotten more so with each passing day.

–from "Reagans Renew Vows for 40th Anniversary," *Los Angeles Times*, March 9, 1992

R ONALD REAGAN COSTARRED WITH JANE WYMAN IN 1938'S *Brother Rat*. He fell in love and soon became engaged with the onetime divorcée, and they were married in January 1940. Maureen was born in 1941, Michael was adopted shortly after his birth, and Christine was born in 1947 and died the same day. With the heartfelt loss of Christine, and Jane's ascending film career, they grew apart and she sued for divorce in 1948, which was granted the next year.

On March 4, 1952, Ronald Reagan married Nancy Davis, "the leading lady of [his] heart." Nancy abandoned her acting career for the traditional family roles of wife and mother. Patricia (Patti) Ann Reagan was born in October 1952 and Ronald (Ron) Prescott Reagan in 1958. Nancy and Ronnie's marriage became an enduring love affair that would last fifty-two years.

★ ★ ★

I more than love you, I'm not whole without you. You are life itself to me. When you are gone I'm waiting for you to return so I can start living again.

—from *I Love You, Ronnie: The Letters of Ronald Reagan to Nancy Reagan,* by Nancy Reagan, a letter to Nancy Reagan from Ronald Reagan on their thirty-first wedding anniversary, March 4, 1983

Did You Know? ★ Jane Wyman (1917–2007) was a singer, dancer, and Academy Award–winning actress. Wyman and Reagan continued to be friends after their divorce. She voted for him in both presidential elections, and she attended Reagan's funeral in 2004 and released a statement acknowledging that "America has lost a great president and a great, kind, and gentle man."

The Reagans (Patti, Nancy, Ronald, Ron, and Michael) in front of their Christmas tree at the Reagans' home in Pacific Palisades, California, 1960.

★ ★ ★

THE GREAT COMMUNICATOR

In our families, and often from our mothers, we first learn about values and caring and the difference between right and wrong. Those of us blessed with loving families draw our confidence from them and the strength we need to face the world. We also first learn at home, and, again, often from our mothers, about the God who will guide us through life.

The mothers we honor this weekend, young or not so young, partners or alone, well-to-do or sometimes agonizingly poor, are as diverse as our varied population. But they share a commitment to future generations and a yearning to improve the world their children will inherit. They shape the America we know today and are now molding the character of our country tomorrow.

Since men seem to have written most of our history books, the role of women and mothers in our communities and families has not always been given its due. But the truth is the wild west could never have been tamed, the vast prairies never plowed, nor God and learning brought to the corners of our continent without the strength, bravery, and influence of our grandmothers, great-grandmothers, and the women who came before them.

Living through blizzards, plagues, prairie fires, and floods, these women made homes and started families, organized churches, and built schools. They served as teachers, field hands, physicians, and the center of the family.

—FROM RADIO ADDRESS TO THE NATION ON THE OBSERVANCE OF
MOTHER'S DAY, MAY 7, 1983

All great change in America begins at the dinner table. So, tomorrow night in the kitchen I hope the talking begins. And children, if your parents haven't been teaching you what it means to be an American, let 'em know and nail 'em on it. That would be a very American thing to do.

—from Farewell Address to the Nation,
January 11, 1989

This is my surprise day. A great luncheon tribute is on for Nancy which I'm not supposed to attend. I will, however. . . . [W]hen she finally appeared to respond to the tribute that had been addressed to her . . . I walked out & on stage spoke my piece. It was a complete surprise to everyone. For once there was no [White House] leak.

—from *The Reagan Diaries*,
August 15, 1988, diary entry

Did You Know? ★ The Reagan ranch in Santa Barbara, California, Rancho del Cielo (Ranch in the Sky), was bought by Ronald and Nancy Reagan in the mid-1970s. Its 688 acres served as their home up until 1995. Reagan spent many enjoyable hours riding, clearing brush, and doing ranch chores. He maintained that the tranquility the ranch provided added years to his life and over the eight years of his presidency, he spent almost a year at Rancho del Cielo.

Nancy and I recently returned from our summer vacation. My horse and I got reacquainted, and I had time to reflect once again on the old truth inherited from the cavalry that there's nothing so good for the inside of a man as the outside of a horse.

—from Q&A session with regional editors and broadcasters,
September 16, 1985

I cite the passage: "And I look to the hills from whence cometh my strength."

—Reagan's response to an interviewer's question regarding his thoughts about the relative isolation of the Reagan ranch,
Santa Barbara News-Press, February 13, 1985

Nancy Davis, seeing the plight of a lonely man who didn't know how lonely he really was, determined to rescue him from a completely empty life. . . . With patience & tenderness she gradually brought the light of understanding to his darkened, obtuse mind and he discovered the joy of loving someone with all his heart.

—from *I Love You, Ronnie*, a letter to Nancy Reagan
from Ronald Reagan, March 4, 1981

The Reagans sitting overlooking Lake Lucky at Rancho del Cielo, California, March 4, 1982.

Lieutenant Ronald Reagan posing with his mother, Nelle, 1940s.

4

Serving His Country

Freedom is never more than one generation away
from extinction. It has to be fought for and defended
by each generation.
— from Annual Convention of Kiwanis International,
July 6, 1987

I
N 1937, REAGAN ENLISTED AS A PRIVATE IN THE ARMY RESERVE
and was quickly promoted to second lieutenant in the
Officers Reserve Corps of the Cavalry. Due to his lifelong
nearsightedness he was not destined to serve overseas, and he
requested assignment to the Army Air Forces, which then posted
him to the First Motion Picture Unit, where he helped make over
four hundred army training films.

Captain Reagan completed his active duty with the end of
World War II.

★ ★ ★

THE GREAT COMMUNICATOR

We are not a warlike people. Quite the opposite. We always seek to live in peace. We resort to force infrequently and with great reluctance—and only after we have determined that it is absolutely necessary. We are awed—and rightly so—by the forces of destruction at loose in the world in this nuclear era. But neither can we be naïve or foolish. Four times in my lifetime America has gone to war, bleeding the lives of its young men into the sands of beachheads, the fields of Europe and the jungles and rice paddies of Asia. We know only too well that war comes not when the forces of freedom are strong, but when they are weak. It is then that tyrants are tempted. We simply cannot learn these lessons the hard way again without risking our destruction.

Of all the objectives we seek, first and foremost is the establishment of lasting world peace. We must always stand ready to negotiate in good faith, ready to pursue any reasonable avenue that holds forth the promise of lessening tensions and furthering the prospects of peace. But let our friends and those who may wish us ill take note: the United States has an obligation to its citizens and to the people of the world never to let those who would destroy freedom dictate the future course of human life on this planet.

—FROM REPUBLICAN NATIONAL CONVENTION
ACCEPTANCE SPEECH, JULY 17, 1980

"Fidelis"—always faithful. Well, the rest of us must remain always faithful to those ideals, which so many have given their lives to protect. Our heritage of liberty must be preserved and passed on. Let no terrorist question our will or no tyrant doubt our resolve. Americans have courage and determination, and we must not and will not be intimidated by anyone, anywhere.

—from remarks to the military personnel at Cherry Point, North Carolina, on the U.S. casualties in Lebanon and Grenada, November 4, 1983

Back in World War II days a young draftee was complaining about some of the methods of the Army and the way the Army did things and was asking an old regular Army sergeant about this. And the regular Army sergeant said, "Son, look, if you were in charge of a brand new country and you were creating your army for that brand new country and you finally got a division created, what would you call it?" And the kid said, "Well, I guess I'd call it the First Division." [The Army sergeant] said, "Well, in the United States they called the first one the Second Division and," he said, "when you understand that, you'll understand everything there is to know about the Army."

—from remarks to American troops at Camp Liberty Bell, Republic of Korea, November 13, 1983

Did You Know? ★ Although off the screen for most of the war, Reagan did act in a few Hollywood films that contributed to the war effort such as 1943's *This Is the Army*, an Irving Berlin musical.

For too long a time, they stood in a chill wind, as if on a winter night's watch. And in that night, their deeds spoke to us, but we knew them not. And their voices called to us, but we heard them not. Yet in this land that God has blessed, the dawn always at last follows the dark, and now morning has come. The night is over. We see these men and know them once again—and know how much we owe them, how much they have given us, and how much we can never fully repay. And not just as individuals, but as a nation, we say we love you.

—from Veterans Day Ceremony at the Vietnam Veterans Memorial, November 11, 1988

Some years ago, I was sent on a mission to Denmark. And while there, I heard stories of the war. And I heard how the order had gone out for the Danish people, under the Nazi occupation, to identify the Jews among them. And the next day, every Dane appeared on the street wearing a Star of David.

—from American Gathering of Jewish Holocaust Survivors, April 11, 1983

WHAT AND WHEN ?

CAPT. R.W. REAGAN

Captain Ronald Reagan in the Army Air Forces working for the First Motion Picture Unit in Culver City, California, 1942–1944.

THE GREAT COMMUNICATOR

The Unknown Soldier who is returned to us today and whom we lay to rest is symbolic of all our missing sons, and we will present him with the Congressional Medal of Honor, the highest military decoration that we can bestow.

About him we may well wonder, as others have: As a child, did he play on some street in a great American city? Or did he work beside his father on a farm out in America's heartland? Did he marry? Did he have children? Did he look expectantly to return to a bride?

We'll never know the answers to these questions about his life. We do know, though, why he died. He saw the horrors of war but bravely faced them, certain his own cause and his country's cause was a noble one; that he was fighting for human dignity, for free men everywhere. Today we pause to embrace him and all who served us so well in a war [Vietnam] whose end offered no parades, no flags, and so little thanks. We can be worthy of the values and ideals for which our sons sacrificed—worthy of their courage in the face of a fear that few of us will ever experience—by honoring their commitment and devotion to duty and country.

—FROM MEMORIAL DAY CEREMONIES, MAY 28, 1984

Ronald Reagan flying a P-40 airplane in a still from the Army Air Forces training film "Identification of a Japanese Zero," 1943.

Some people think of members of the military as only warriors, fierce in their martial expertise. But the men and women we mourn today were peacemakers. They were there to protect life and preserve a peace, to act as a force for stability and hope and trust. Their commitment was as strong as their purpose was pure. And they were proud. They had a rendezvous with destiny and a potential they never failed to meet.

—from memorial service in Fort Campbell, Kentucky, for members of the 101st Airborne Division who died in a Newfoundland airplane crash, December 16, 1985

You know, throughout my life, I've seen America do the impossible. We survived a Great Depression that toppled many governments throughout the world. We came back from Pearl Harbor to win the greatest military victory in world history. In a single lifetime, my own, we have gone from horse and buggy to sending astronauts to the Moon.

We, as Americans, have fought harder, we've paid a higher price, done more to advance the freedom and dignity of man than any other people who ever lived on this Earth.

Ours is the land of the free because it is the home of the brave. And America's future will always be great because our nation will be strong. And our people will be free because we will be united—one people, under God, with liberty and justice for all.

—from Reagan-Bush Rally, Boston, Massachusetts, November 1, 1984

★★★

Forty summers have passed since the battle that you fought here. You were young the day you took these cliffs; some of you were hardly more than boys, with the deepest joys of life before you. Yet, you risked everything here. Why? Why did you do it? What impelled you to put aside the instinct for self-preservation and risk your lives to take these cliffs? What inspired all the men of the armies that met here? We look at you, and somehow we know the answer. It was faith and belief; it was loyalty and love.

The men of Normandy had faith that what they were doing was right, faith that they fought for all humanity, faith that a just God would grant them mercy on this beachhead or on the next. It was the deep knowledge—and pray God we have not lost it—that there is a profound, moral difference between the use of force for liberation and the use of force for conquest. You were here to liberate, not to conquer, and so you and those others did not doubt your cause. And you were right not to doubt. . . . The Americans who fought here that morning knew word of the invasion was spreading through the darkness back home. They fought—or felt in their hearts, though they couldn't know in fact, that in Georgia they were filling the churches at 4 a.m., in Kansas they were kneeling on their porches and praying, and in Philadelphia they were ringing the Liberty Bell.

—FROM 40TH ANNIVERSARY OF THE NORMANDY INVASION,
D-DAY, JUNE 6, 1984

We will always remember. We will always be proud. We will always be prepared, so we may always be free.

—from 40th Anniversary of the Normandy Invasion, D-Day, June 6, 1984

Everywhere here are memories—pulling us, touching us, making us understand that they can never be erased. Such memories take us where God intended His children to go—toward learning, toward healing, and, above all, toward redemption. They beckon us through the endless stretches of our heart to the knowing commitment that the life of each individual can change the world and make it better.

We're all witnesses; we share the glistening hope that rests in every human soul. Hope leads us, if we're prepared to trust it, toward what our President Lincoln called the better angels of our nature. And then, rising above all this cruelty, out of this tragic and nightmarish time, beyond the anguish, the pain and the suffering for all time, we can and must pledge: Never again.

—from commemorative ceremony at Bergen-Belsen Concentration Camp in the Federal Republic of Germany, May 5, 1985

People do not make wars; governments do.

—from Q&A with the students and faculty at Moscow State University, May 31, 1988

THE STORYTELLER

'm thinking of one special story—that of a mother and her young son living alone in a modest cottage in the middle of the woods. And one night as the Battle of the Bulge exploded not far away, and around them, three young American soldiers arrived at their door—they were standing there in the snow, lost behind enemy lines. All were frostbitten; one was badly wounded. Even though sheltering the enemy was punishable by death, she took them in and made them a supper with some of her last food. Then, they heard another knock at the door. And this time four German soldiers stood there. The woman was afraid, but she quickly said with a firm voice, "There will be no shooting here." She made all the soldiers lay down their weapons, and they all joined in the makeshift meal. . . .

That night—as the storm of war tossed the world—they had their own private armistice. And the next morning, the German corporal showed the Americans how to get back behind their own lines. And they all shook hands and went their separate ways. That happened to be Christmas Day, forty years ago.

Those boys reconciled briefly in the midst of war. Surely we allies in peacetime should honor the reconciliation of the last forty years.

—FROM CEREMONY AT BITBURG AIR BASE IN THE
FEDERAL REPUBLIC OF GERMANY, MAY 5, 1985

The Reagans aboard a boat in California, 1964.

When I was Governor, back in those days of the riots on the campus and all that was going on, I wanted more than anything to be able to go to the campus and talk to some of those young people, but if I went I started a riot. I was the establishment. And one day some of the student leaders in our university system in California demanded a meeting with me. Well, I was delighted.

And they came in and, as was the custom of some in that day, in torn T-shirts and some of them barefoot, slouched into their chairs, and then one of the spokesmen teed off, and he started in on me. And he said, "You know, Governor, it's impossible for you to understand your own children." He said, "Your generation cannot understand ours at all." Well, I tried to pass it off. I said, "We know more about being young than we do about being old."

And he said, "No, I'm serious." He said, "When you were our age, when you were growing up," he said, "you didn't have instant electronics, computers figuring in seconds what it used to take months and weeks or days to compute." He said, "You didn't have jet travel. You didn't have space exploration." And he went on like that. And, you know, usually you only get the right answer after it's over and you've gone home, but he talked just long enough that the Lord blessed me, and I thought of the answer. And when he paused for breath, I said, "You're absolutely right. We didn't have those things when we were your age. We invented them."

—from White House briefing for the
National Alliance of Senior Citizens, February 29, 1984

I would like to be president, because I would like to see this country become once again a country where a little six-year-old girl can grow up knowing the same freedom that I knew when I was six years old, growing up in America.

—from "To Restore America" (Reagan's Campaign Address),
March 31, 1976

We, as a people, aren't happy if we are not moving forward. A nation that is growing and thriving is one which will solve its problems. We must offer progress instead of stagnation; the truth instead of promises; hope and faith instead of defeatism and despair. Then, I am sure, the people will make those decisions which will restore confidence in our way of life and release that energy that is the American spirit.

—from announcement for 1976 presidential candidacy,
November 20, 1975

No people who have ever lived on this earth have fought harder, paid a higher price for freedom, or done more to advance the dignity of man than the living Americans—the Americans living in this land today. There isn't any problem we can't solve if government will give us the facts. Tell us what needs to be done. Then, get out of the way and let us have at it.

—from "To Restore America" (Reagan's Campaign Address),
March 31, 1976

I am paying for this microphone. . . .

> —from Republican presidential debate, Nashua,
> New Hampshire, February 23, 1980, in response to
> the moderator who was ordering the sound engineer
> to "turn Mr. Reagan's mic off!" (Reagan was understandably
> annoyed as his campaign had paid the debate costs)

Did You Know? ★ Reagan later mused that his snappy riposte of "I am paying for this microphone" may have won him the debate, the primary—and the nomination.

A recession is when your neighbor loses his job. A depression is when you lose yours. Recovery is when Jimmy Carter loses his.

> —from Labor Day speech at Liberty State Park,
> Jersey City, New Jersey, September 1, 1980

There you go again.

> —from the only presidential debate between President
> Jimmy Carter and Ronald Reagan, just a week before the
> election, Cleveland, Ohio, Convention Center Music Hall,
> October 28, 1980

Did You Know? ★ Reagan's "There you go again" phrase was funny and underscored in a gentle, mocking way President Jimmy Carter's dwelling on rehashed issues. The phrase would go on to become a common retort in future political debates, used or paraphrased by the likes of Sarah Palin and Bill Clinton.

Next Tuesday is election day. Next Tuesday all of you will go to the polls; you'll stand there in the polling place and make a decision. I think when you make that decision, it might be well if you would ask yourself, are you better off than you were four years ago? Is it easier for you to go and buy things in the stores than it was four years ago? Is there more or less unemployment in the country than there was four years ago? Is America as respected throughout the world as it was? Do you feel that our security is as safe, that we're as strong as we were four years ago? And if you answer all of those questions yes, why then, I think your choice is very obvious as to who you'll vote for. If you don't agree, if you don't think that this course that we've been on for the last four years is what you would like to see us follow for the next four, then I could suggest another choice that you have.

  —from the only presidential debate between President Jimmy Carter and Ronald Reagan, just a week before the election, Cleveland, Ohio, Convention Center Music Hall, October 28, 1980

★ ★ ★

THE GREAT COMMUNICATOR

I believe this nation hungers for a spiritual revival; hungers to once again see honor placed above political expediency; to see government once again the protector of our liberties, not the distributor of gifts and privilege. Government should uphold and not undermine those institutions, which are custodians of the very values upon which civilization is founded—religion, education and, above all, family. Government cannot be clergyman, teacher, and parent. It is our servant, beholden to us.

We who are privileged to be Americans have had a rendezvous with destiny since the moment in 1630 when John Winthrop, standing on the deck of the tiny *Arabella* off the coast of Massachusetts, told the little band of pilgrims, "We shall be as a city upon a hill. The eyes of all people are upon us so that if we shall deal falsely with our God in this work we have undertaken and so cause Him to withdraw His present help from us, we shall be made a story and a byword throughout the world."

A troubled and afflicted mankind looks to us, pleading for us to keep our rendezvous with destiny; that we will uphold the principles of self-reliance, self-discipline, morality, and—above all—responsible liberty for every individual that we will become that shining city on a hill.

I believe that you and I together can keep this rendezvous with destiny.

—FROM ANNOUNCEMENT FOR 1980 PRESIDENTIAL CANDIDACY,
NOVEMBER 13, 1979

Back in the States, we're terribly proud of anything more than a few hundred years old; some even see my election to the Presidency as America's attempt to show our European cousins that we, too, have a regard for antiquity.

—from remarks to members of the
Royal Institute of International Affairs in London, June 3, 1988
(Reagan often used the fact of his advanced age in a humorous
and self-deprecating way that often proved disarming)

I have a good makeup team. It's the same people who've been repairing the Statue of Liberty.

—from Annual White House News Photographers' Association
Dinner, May 15, 1986

You know, it's always great to be in Florida, but it's not true that I keep returning just because Ponce de Leon thought that this was the place to find the Fountain of Youth. The fact is Ponce de Leon never did find the Fountain of Youth. I know, I was with him on that trip.

—from fund-raising luncheon for Representative Connie Mack,
Miami, Florida, June 29, 1988

Ronald Reagan giving his acceptance speech at the Republican National Convention, Detroit, Michigan, July 17, 1980.

Waving from the limousine during the Inaugural Parade, Washington, DC, January 20, 1981.

6

Fortieth President of the United States

FIRST TERM: 1981–1982

Let us so conduct ourselves that two centuries from now, another Congress and another President, meeting in this Chamber as we are meeting, will speak of us with pride, saying that we met the test and preserved for them in their day the sacred flame of liberty—this last, best hope of man on Earth.

—from State of the Union Address, January 26, 1982

CITIZEN RONALD REAGAN TOOK THE OATH OF OFFICE OF President of the United States on January 20, 1981, inheriting high interest rates, double-digit inflation, and the worst economic recession since the Great Depression, and in his address to the nation that followed his swearing in, the fortieth President promised fiscal renewal by promoting American initiative and enterprise by laissez-faire philosophy and deregulating the federal government to allow free market capitalism. The Reagan Revolution that would ensue would raise the national morale from a decade-long malaise, typified by the Vietnam War, Watergate, Soviet expansion, and big government. On the same day as the inauguration, after 444 days of captivity, Iran released the fifty-two American hostages that it had held in the U.S. embassy in Tehran. There was a growing feeling of optimism that this was a President who could get things done.

On March 30, 1981, as President Reagan left a speaking engagement in Washington, DC, and prepared to get into the presidential limousine, John Hinckley Jr. stepped out and fired six shots, two of which wounded the President, one in his lower right arm and one in his left lung, an inch from his heart. (Three others were also hit by bullets, including White House Press Secretary James Brady, who remained partially paralyzed after his recovery.) Hinckley was quickly subdued and President Reagan was sped to George Washington University Hospital and into surgery.

Reagan made a full recovery a month later and appeared before Congress to a hero's welcome. In his first year in office he oversaw congressional passage of his tax bill, which cut the rate 25 percent; gave an ultimatum to striking air traffic controllers to either go back to work or be fired, which broke the union strike; and made history by appointing the first female Supreme Court justice, Sandra Day O'Connor.

President Reagan waving to the crowd immediately before being shot in an assassination attempt, Washington Hilton Hotel, March 30, 1981.

Chaos outside the Washington Hilton Hotel after the assassination attempt on President Reagan. James Brady and police officer Thomas Delahanty (foreground) lie wounded on the ground, March 30, 1981.

President Reagan giving the Inaugural Address from the U.S. Capitol, January 20, 1981.

In June 1982 he addressed the British House of Commons and predicted that Marxism-Leninism would end up "on the ash-heap of history," and in the fall the United States experienced a brief recession, the unemployment rate went up, and there was a tremendous projected budget gap, but Reagan refused to raise taxes or cut defense spending.

★ ★ ★

The economic ills we suffer have come upon us over several decades. They will not go away in days, weeks, or months, but they will go away. They will go away because we as Americans have the capacity now, as we've had in the past, to do whatever needs to be done to preserve this last and greatest bastion of freedom. In this present crisis, government is not the solution to our problem; government is the problem. From time to time we've been tempted to believe that society has become too complex to be managed by self-rule, that government by an elite group is superior to government for, by, and of the people. Well, if no one among us is capable of governing himself, then who among us has the capacity to govern someone else? All of us together, in and out of government, must bear the burden. . . .

Progress may be slow, measured in inches and feet, not miles, but we will progress.

—from First Presidential Inaugural Address,
January 20, 1981

The best view of big government is in the rearview mirror as we leave it behind.

—from Spirit of America Rally, Atlanta, Georgia,
January 26, 1984

The nine most terrifying words in the English language are: "I'm from the government and I'm here to help."

—from President's press conference, August 12, 1986

"We the People" tell the government what to do; it doesn't tell us. "We the People" are the driver; the government is the car. And we decide where it should go, and by what route, and how fast. Almost all the world's constitutions are documents in which governments tell the people what their privileges are. Our Constitution is a document in which "We the People" tell the government what it is allowed to do. "We the People" are free.

—from Farewell Address to the Nation,
January 11, 1989

I often reflect that it was not too long ago when sand was just the stuff beaches were made of. In fact, one of the lines in my old speeches said if we put the government in charge of sand, there'd be a shortage.

—from Presentation Ceremony for the National Medals of Science and Technology, July 15, 1988

The Reagans in the presidential limousine during the Inaugural Parade, Washington, DC, January 20, 1981.

THE GREAT COMMUNICATOR

We have every right to dream heroic dreams. Those who say that we are in a time when there are no heroes, they just don't know where to look. You can see heroes every day going in and out of factory gates. Others, a handful in number, produce enough food to feed all of us and then the world beyond. You meet heroes across a counter, and they're on both sides of that counter. There are entrepreneurs with faith in themselves and faith in an idea who create new jobs, new wealth and opportunity. They're individuals and families whose taxes support the government and whose voluntary gifts support church, charity, culture, art, and education. Their patriotism is quiet, but deep. Their values sustain our national life.

Now, I have used the words "they" and "their" in speaking of these heroes. I could say "you" and "your'" because I'm addressing the heroes of whom I speak—you, the citizens of this blessed land. Your dreams, your hopes, your goals are going to be the dreams, the hopes, and the goals of this administration, so help me God.

We shall reflect the compassion that is so much a part of your makeup. How can we love our country and not love our countrymen; and loving them, reach out a hand when they fall, heal them when they're sick, and provide opportunity to make them self-sufficient so they will be equal in fact and not just in theory?

—FROM FIRST PRESIDENTIAL INAUGURAL ADDRESS, JANUARY 20, 1981

Government can create opportunities by knocking down unfair barriers, but businesses themselves must follow through with the proposals, creativity, and workmanship that made America the leader in this field.

> —from White House meeting with the Associated General Contractors of America, April 18, 1988

There's an old story about a town—it could be anywhere—with a bureaucrat who is known to be a good-for-nothing, but he somehow had always hung on to power. So one day, in a town meeting, an old woman got up and said to him: "There is a folk legend here where I come from that when a baby is born, an angel comes down from heaven and kisses it on one part of its body. If the angel kisses him on his hand, he becomes a handyman. If he kisses him on his forehead, he becomes bright and clever. And I've been trying to figure out where the angel kissed you so that you should sit there for so long and do nothing."

> —from Q&A with the students and faculty at Moscow State University, May 31, 1988

[Reaganomics] sounds like a fad diet or an aerobic exercise.

> —from February 5, 1983 radio speech, *Ronald Reagan: The Presidential Portfolio*

*President Reagan working in his state room aboard
Air Force One on a trip to France, June 2, 1982.*

As Carl Sandburg said, all we need to begin with is a dream that we can do better than before. All we need to have is faith, and that dream will come true. All we need to do is act, and the time for action is now.

—from Address before Congress,
April 28, 1981

You have the right to dream great dreams. You have the right to seek a better world for your people. And all of us have the responsibility to work for that better world. And as caring, peaceful peoples, think what a powerful force for good we could be.

—from 38th Session of the UN General Assembly,
New York, September 26, 1983

Today's young Americans will come into their own with freedom, know-how, and resources far beyond anything the world has ever known. . . . We've got every reason to look to the future with unbounding optimism. Today a refreshing breeze can be felt across the face of mankind. Winds of freedom are blowing, clearing the air, opening the view of a new and wondrous horizon.

In a few days, Nancy and I . . . will be heading west . . . And as we liftoff aboard *Air Force One*, circling half the globe, the winds of freedom will be propelling my mission.

—from the International Forum of the Chamber of Commerce
of the United States, April 23, 1986

"Honey," I said, "I forgot to duck."
—from *An American Life*, Ronald Reagan's comment to
Nancy Reagan after assassination attempt
on March 30, 1981

Getting shot hurts.
—from *The Reagan Diaries*, March 30, 1981, diary entry

Did You Know? ★ After the assassination attempt, Reagan
reportedly removed his oxygen mask while in the operating
room before his surgery and said: "I hope you are all Republicans." One of the doctors, a Democrat, replied: "Today, Mr.
President, we are all Republicans."

Death and taxes may be inevitable, but unjust taxes are not.
The first American Revolution was sparked by an unshakable
conviction—taxation without representation is tyranny.
—from Address to the Nation, May 28, 1985

If I could paraphrase a well-known statement by Will Rogers that
he had never met a man he didn't like, I'm afraid we have some
people around here who never met a tax they didn't hike.
—from Address to the Nation, July 27, 1981

This is my second visit to Great Britain as President of the United States. My first opportunity to stand on British soil occurred almost a year and a half ago when your Prime Minister graciously hosted a diplomatic dinner at the British Embassy in Washington. Mrs. Thatcher said then that she hoped I was not distressed to find staring down at me from the grand staircase a portrait of His Royal Majesty King George III. She suggested it was best to let bygones be bygones, and in view of our two countries' remarkable friendship in succeeding years, she added that most Englishmen today would agree with Thomas Jefferson that "a little rebellion now and then is a very good thing."

—from Westminster speech delivered
to the British House of Commons, June 4, 1982

Did You Know? ★ Margaret Hilda Thatcher (1925–2013) first met Governor Reagan in 1975 and their mutual conservative philosophy made them political soul mates. With Reagan's election as President in 1980 the two world leaders pursued a mutual agenda of encouraging free markets, cutting taxes, and taking a tough stance against unions and communism, which led to a personal, close friendship. At Reagan's funeral Thatcher said, "We have lost a great president, a great American, and a great man. And I have lost a dear friend."

THE STORYTELLER

But the joke that I was going to tell you was a little story that took place in ancient Rome at the Coliseum. A little band of Christians out there in the sand on the floor of the Coliseum, crowd up there in the seats, and then they were going to turn the lions loose on them. And they did. And the lions came roaring out and charging down on this little huddled mass of people. And one of them stepped forward and said a few quiet words, and the lion stopped and laid down. Well, the crowd was enraged that they weren't going to get the show that they'd expected. Caesar was so mad that he had them bring the man to him, and he said, "What did you say that made the lions act like that?" [The man] said, "I just told them that after they ate there would be speeches."

—FROM REPUBLICAN GOVERNORS CLUB ANNUAL DINNER,
OCTOBER 15, 1987

I've said before, balancing the budget is a little like protecting your virtue: You just have to learn to say "no."

—from Kansas State University at the Alfred M. Landon Lecture Series on Public Issues, September 9, 1982

Facts are stupid things—stubborn things, I should say.

—from Republican National Convention in New Orleans, Louisiana, August 15, 1988

Today marks my first State of the Union address to you, a constitutional duty as old as our Republic itself.

President Washington began this tradition in 1790 after reminding the Nation that the destiny of self-government and the "preservation of the sacred fire of liberty" is "finally staked on the experiment entrusted to the hands of the American people." For our friends in the press, who place a high premium on accuracy, let me say: I did not actually hear George Washington say that. But it is a matter of historic record.

—from State of the Union Address, January 26, 1982

Do we tell these Americans to give up hope, that their ship of state lies dead in the water because those entrusted with manning that ship can't agree on which sail to raise? We're within sight of the safe port of economic recovery. Do we make port or go aground on the shoals of selfishness, partisanship, and just plain bullheadedness?

—from Address to the Nation, August 16, 1982

They say that money talks. Well, a few years ago the only thing it said was good-bye.

—from fund-raising dinner for Senator Mack Mattingly, Atlanta, Georgia, June 5, 1985

What I am describing now is a plan and a hope for the long term—the march of freedom and democracy which will leave Marxism-Leninism on the ash-heap of history as it has left other tyrannies which stifle the freedom and muzzle the self-expression of the people.

—from Westminster speech delivered to the British House of Commons, June 4, 1982

"We must learn to live together in peace," [President Harry Truman] said. "We must build a new world—a far better world." What a better world it would be if the guns were silent, if neighbor no longer encroached on neighbor, and all peoples were free to reap the rewards of their toil and determine their own destiny and system of government, whatever their choice.

—from UN General Assembly special session devoted to disarmament, New York, June 17, 1982

Tragic turmoil in the Middle East runs back to the dawn of history. In our modern day, conflict after conflict has taken its brutal toll there. In an age of nuclear challenge and economic interdependence, such conflicts are a threat to all the people of the world, not just the Middle East itself. It's time for us all—in the Middle East and around the world—to call a halt to conflict, hatred, and prejudice. It's time for us all to launch a common effort for reconstruction, peace, and progress.

—from Address to the Nation, September 1, 1982

Peace is more than just an absence of war. True peace is justice, true peace is freedom, and true peace dictates the recognition of human rights.

—from 41st Session of the UN General Assembly, New York, September 22, 1986

Funny—I was talking peace but wearing a bullet proof vest.

—from *The Reagan Diaries*, November 18, 1981, diary entry

You can tell a lot about a fellow's character by his way of eating jellybeans.

—quoted in *Observer*, March 29, 1981

Did You Know? ★ In 1966 while running for the Governor of California and in what proved a successful method of giving up pipe smoking Reagan started eating Goelitz Mini Jelly Beans and the company began a years-long monthly shipment to the Governor's Mansion and then later to the White House. For the Inaugural in 1981 the company shipped three and a half tons of red, white, and blue Jelly Belly jellybeans to Washington and a jar of jellybeans would become a mainstay on the Cabinet table in the White House. Reagan's favorite flavor was licorice.

President Reagan addressing the Annual Convention of the National Association of Evangelicals ("Evil Empire" speech) in Orlando, Florida, March 8, 1983.

7

Star Wars and the Evil Empire

FIRST TERM: 1983–1984

America is too great for small dreams. There was a
hunger in the land for a spiritual revival; if you will, a
crusade for renewal. The American people said: Let us
look to the future with confidence, both at home and
abroad. Let us give freedom a chance.

— from State of the Union Address, January 25, 1984

IN MARCH 1983 REAGAN PROMOTED RESEARCH AND DEVELOPMENT
of the Strategic Defense Initiative (SDI), dubbed "Star Wars"
by its detractors, which was a proposed land-and-space-
based antiballistic missile system meant to change the nuclear
war deterrent dynamic from an offensive strategy, also known as
Mutual Assured Destruction (MAD), to a more sensible defensive
strategy. The Soviets viewed SDI, even if it might not be realizable
for many years, as an intensification of the arms race because it

would neutralize their missiles, leaving them defenseless to a U.S. intercontinental ballistic missile strike. During 1984 Reagan sought to negotiate a reduction of nuclear weapons with the Soviet Union but met with resistance and suspicion. In a further move to promote the Reagan Doctrine, to confront, contain, and deter communist imperialism, he supported aid to the Contras fighting in Nicaragua.

The Democratic nominee for the presidential election of 1984 was Walter Mondale, but Mondale's vow to raise taxes in the face of the economic turnaround created by Reagan's fiscal policy and Reagan's popular appeal made Reagan's reelection likely. But Reagan's poor performance in his first debate with Mondale raised questions about his age. His vigor and wit in the second debate put that issue to rest, though, and Reagan won the election with a greater electoral landslide, 525 to 49, than he had reaped four years earlier, and he won 59 percent of the popular vote.

★ ★ ★

Governments got in the way of the dreams of the people. Dreams became issues of East versus West. Hopes became political rhetoric. Progress became a search for power and domination. Somewhere the truth was lost that people don't make wars, governments do.

—from 38th Session of the UN General Assembly, New York,
September 26, 1983

President Reagan addressing U.S. troops at Camp Liberty Bell,
the DMZ, Republic of Korea, November 13, 1983.

But if history teaches anything, it teaches that simple-minded appeasement or wishful thinking about our adversaries is folly. It means the betrayal of our past, the squandering of our freedom.

So, I urge you to speak out against those who would place the United States in a position of military and moral inferiority . . . So, in your discussions of the nuclear freeze proposals, I urge you to beware the temptation of pride—the temptation of blithely declaring yourselves above it all and label both sides equally at fault, to ignore the facts of history and the aggressive impulses of an evil empire, to simply call the arms race a giant misunderstanding and thereby remove yourself from the struggle between right and wrong and good and evil.

I ask you to resist the attempts of those who would have you withhold your support for our efforts, this administration's efforts, to keep America strong and free, while we negotiate real and verifiable reductions in the world's nuclear arsenals and one day, with God's help, their total elimination.

While America's military strength is important, let me add here that I've always maintained that the struggle now going on for the world will never be decided by bombs or rockets, by armies or military might. The real crisis we face today is a spiritual one; at root, it is a test of moral will and faith.

—FROM ANNUAL CONVENTION OF THE NATIONAL ASSOCIATION OF EVANGELICALS ("EVIL EMPIRE" SPEECH), ORLANDO, FLORIDA, MARCH 8, 1983

History is not a darkening path twisting inevitably toward tyranny, as the forces of totalitarianism would have us believe. Indeed, the one clear pattern in world events—a pattern that's grown with each passing year of this century—is in the opposite direction.

It is the growing determination of men and women of all races and conditions to gain control of their own destinies and to free themselves from arbitrary domination. More than any other single force, this is the driving aspiration that unites the human family today—the burning desire to live unhindered in a world that respects the rights of individuals and nations.

—from Annual Washington Conference of the American Legion,

February 22, 1983

The joke they tell is that an American and a Russian were arguing about the differences between our two countries. And the American said, "Look, in my country I can walk into the Oval Office; I can hit the desk with my fist and say, 'President Reagan, I don't like the way you're governing the United States.'" And the Russian said, "I can do that." The American said, "What?" He says, "I can walk into the Kremlin, into Brezhnev's office. I can pound Brezhnev's desk, and I can say, 'Mr. President, I don't like the way Ronald Reagan is governing the United States.'"

—from commencement exercises at Eureka College,

May 9, 1982

THE GREAT COMMUNICATOR

Let me share with you a vision of the future, which offers hope. It is that we embark on a program to counter the awesome Soviet missile threat with measures that are defensive. Let us turn to the very strengths in technology that spawned our great industrial base and that have given us the quality of life we enjoy today.

What if free people could live secure in the knowledge that their security did not rest upon the threat of instant U.S. retaliation to deter a Soviet attack, that we could intercept and destroy strategic ballistic missiles before they reached our own soil or that of our allies?

I know this is a formidable, technical task, one that may not be accomplished before the end of this century. Yet, current technology has attained a level of sophistication where it's reasonable for us to begin this effort. It will take years, probably decades of effort on many fronts. There will be failures and setbacks, just as there will be successes and breakthroughs. And as we proceed, we must remain constant in preserving the nuclear deterrent and maintaining a solid capability for flexible response. But isn't it worth every investment necessary to free the world from the threat of nuclear war? We know it is.

—FROM ADDRESS TO THE NATION ("STAR WARS" SPEECH),
MARCH 23, 1983

We preach no manifest destiny. But like Americans who began this country and brought forth this last, best hope of mankind, history has asked much of the Americans of our own time. Much we have already given; much more we must be prepared to give.

—from Address to the Nation on a Soviet jet fighter shooting down civilian Korean Air Lines Flight 007 on September 1, 1983, killing all 269 people on board, September 5, 1983

We're a nation with global responsibilities. We're not somewhere else in the world protecting someone else's interests; we're there protecting our own.

—from Address to the Nation on events in Lebanon and Grenada, October 27, 1983

Did You Know? ★ On October 23, 1983, a suicide bomber crashed into the U.S. Marine barracks in Beirut in a truck loaded with high explosives, and 241 were killed. Two days later, in response to a leftist countercoup on the island nation of Grenada, U.S. troops invaded and deposed the regime, allowing parliamentary elections to elect a new prime minister.

We owe it to the unfortunate to be aware of their plight and to help them in every way we can. No one can quarrel with that. We must and do have compassion for all the victims of this economic crisis. But the big story about America today is the way that millions of confident, caring people—those extraordinary "ordinary" Americans who never make the headlines and will never be interviewed—are laying the foundation, not just for recovery from our present problems but for a better tomorrow for all our people.

From coast to coast, on the job and in classrooms and laboratories, at new construction sites and in churches and community groups, neighbors are helping neighbors. And they've already begun the building, the research, the work, and the giving that will make our country great again.

I believe this, because I believe in them—in the strength of their hearts and minds, in the commitment that each one of them brings to their daily lives, be they high or humble. The challenge for us in government is to be worthy of them—to make government a help, not a hindrance to our people in the challenging but promising days ahead.

If we do that, if we care what our children and our children's children will say of us, if we want them one day to be thankful for what we did here in these temples of freedom, we will work together to make America better for our having been here—not just in this year or this decade but in the next century and beyond.

—from State of the Union Address, January 25, 1983

Now our nation has decided to honor Dr. Martin Luther King Jr.,
by setting aside a day each year to remember him and the just
cause he stood for. We've made historic strides since Rosa Parks
refused to go to the back of the bus. As a democratic people, we
can take pride in the knowledge that we Americans recognized
a grave injustice and took action to correct it. And we should
remember that in far too many countries, people like Dr. King
never have the opportunity to speak out at all.

But traces of bigotry still mar America. So, each year on Martin
Luther King Day, let us not only recall Dr. King, but rededicate
ourselves to the Commandments he believed in and sought to
live every day: Thou shall love thy God with all thy heart, and
thou shall love thy neighbor as thyself.

—from signing of the bill making the birthday of
Martin Luther King Jr. a national holiday,
November 2, 1983

We must never remain silent in the face of bigotry. We must
condemn those who seek to divide us. In all quarters and at
all times, we must teach tolerance and denounce racism, anti-
Semitism, and all ethnic or religious bigotry wherever they exist
as unacceptable evils. We have no place for haters in America—
none, whatsoever.

—from remarks to members of the congregation of Temple Hill
and Jewish community leaders, Valley Stream,
New York, October 26, 1984

As an older American, I remember a time when people of different race, creed, or ethnic origin in our land found hatred and prejudice installed in social custom and, yes, in law. There's no story more heartening in our history than the progress that we've made toward the brotherhood of man that God intended for us. Let us resolve there will be no turning back or hesitation on the road to an America rich in dignity and abundant with opportunity for all our citizens.

Let us resolve that we, the people, will build an American opportunity society in which all of us—white and black, rich and poor, young and old—will go forward together, arm in arm. Again, let us remember that though our heritage is one of blood lines from every corner of the Earth, we are all Americans, pledged to carry on this last, best hope of man on Earth.

—from Second Presidential Inaugural Address, January 21, 1985

Call it mysticism if you will, I have always believed there was some divine providence that placed this great land here between the two great oceans, to be found by a special kind of people from every corner of the world, who had a special love for freedom and a special courage that enabled them to leave their own land, leave their friends and their countrymen, and come to this new and strange land to build a New World of peace and freedom and hope.

—from Statue of Liberty Centennial Celebration,
New York, July 3, 1986

Y ou know, back in the days of vaudeville, vaudevillians trying to get bookings and even young ones trying to break into the show business would go into an empty theater, and there'd be an agent sitting out there in about the third row, all alone in the theater, cigar in his mouth, wearing a check suit, and the vaudevillian would have to show his wares to this cynic.

And one day a young fellow came in—the agent was sitting out there—and this young fellow who wanted to break into show business walked down to the stage and the agent said, "All right, kid, what do you do?"

And the kid never answered. He just took off and flew around the ceiling of the theater, made a couple of circles right up there at the top, and then zoomed down and stopped right in front of the agent.

The agent took the cigar out of his mouth and says, "What else do you do besides bird imitations?"

Well, I've felt that way quite a bit about some of the people that were so critical of what we were trying to do here. There are still some of them around, and they think what we're doing are bird imitations.

—FROM WHITE HOUSE MEETING WITH THE
AMERICAN RETAIL FEDERATION, MAY 16, 1984

History is the work of free men and women, not unalterable laws. It is never inevitable, but it does have directions and trends; and one trend is clear—democracies are not only increasing in number, they're growing in strength. Today they're strong enough to give the cause of freedom growing room and breathing space, and that's all that freedom ever really needs. "The mass of mankind has not been born with saddles on their backs." Thomas Jefferson said that. Freedom is the flagship of the future and the flashfire of the future. Its spark ignites the deepest and noblest aspirations of the human soul.

Those who think the Western democracies are trying to roll back history are missing the point. History is moving in the direction of self-government and the human dignity that it institutionalizes, and the future belongs to the free.

—from address before the Irish National Parliament,
June 4, 1984

I want you to know that . . . I will not make age an issue of this campaign. I am not going to exploit for political purposes, my opponent's youth and inexperience.

—from presidential debate between President Ronald Reagan and Walter Mondale, October 8, 1984, Reagan's reply when asked by the moderator if he as the oldest U.S. President in history would be able to function in the event of a crisis in a second term

In 1980 we asked the people of America, "Are you better off than you were four years ago?" Well, the people answered then by choosing us to bring about a change. . . . Let us ask for their help again . . . to move us further forward on the road we presently travel, the road of common sense, of people in control of their own destiny; the road leading to prosperity and economic expansion in a world at peace.

—from presidential nomination acceptance speech,
Republican National Convention, August 23, 1984

One of my favorite quotations about age comes from Thomas Jefferson. He said that we should never judge a President by his age, only by his work. And ever since he told me that—I've stopped worrying. And just to show you how youthful I am, I intend to campaign in all thirteen States.

—from White House briefing for the
National Alliance of Senior Citizens, February 29, 1984

You know, in our debate, I got a little angry all those times that he distorted my record. And on one occasion, I was about to say to him very sternly, "Mr. Mondale, you're taxing my patience." Then I caught myself. Why should I give him another idea? That's the only tax he hasn't thought of.

—from comment made during a whistlestop tour,
Ottawa, Ohio, October 12, 1984

Just this past Fourth of July, the torch atop the Statue of Liberty was hoisted down for replacement. We can be forgiven for thinking that maybe it was just worn out from lighting the way to freedom for 17 million new Americans. So, now we'll put up a new one.

The poet called Miss Liberty's torch the "lamp beside the golden door." Well, that was the entrance to America, and it still is. And now you really know why we're here tonight.

The glistening hope of that lamp is still ours. Every promise, every opportunity is still golden in this land. And through that golden door our children can walk into tomorrow with the knowledge that no one can be denied the promise that is America.

Her heart is full; her door is still golden, her future bright. She has arms big enough to comfort and strong enough to support, for the strength in her arms is the strength of her people. She will carry on in the eighties unafraid, unashamed, and unsurpassed.

In this springtime of hope, some lights seem eternal; America's is.

—from presidential nomination acceptance speech,

Republican National Convention,

August 23, 1984

President Reagan and Nancy Reagan attending the memorial service for Lebanon and Grenada casualties, Camp Lejeune, North Carolina, November 4, 1983.

America's best days are yet to come. And I know it may drive my opponents up the wall, but I'm going to say it anyway: You ain't seen nothin' yet.

— from Reagan-Bush Rally in Fairfield, Connecticut, October 26, 1984

I've never felt more strongly that America's best days and democracy's best days lie ahead. We're a powerful force for good. With faith and courage, we can perform great deeds and take freedom's next step. And we will. We will carry on the tradition of a good and worthy people who have brought light where there was darkness, warmth where there was cold, medicine where there was disease, food where there was hunger, and peace where there was only bloodshed.

Let us be sure that those who come after will say of us in our time, that in our time we did everything that could be done. We finished the race; we kept them free; we kept the faith.

— from State of the Union Address, January 25, 1984

President Reagan and Nancy Reagan on the Great Wall of China, April 29, 1984.

President Reagan giving his acceptance speech at the Republican National Convention, Dallas, Texas, August 23, 1984.

8

It's Morning in America Again
SECOND TERM: 1985–1986

We stand at a crossroads. The hour is late, the task is
large, and the stakes are momentous.

> —from Address to the Nation, April 24, 1985

A T AGE SEVENTY-THREE, RONALD REAGAN BECAME THE
oldest President to be sworn into office. In November
1985 Reagan met with Mikhail Gorbachev, the Soviet
leader, in Geneva to negotiate a reduction of nuclear arsenals by 50
percent, but no negotiation was reached because Reagan refused
to compromise on his SDI strategy. A further Reagan-Gorbachev
meeting on reducing missiles broke down in Reykjavik, Iceland,
with Reagan again refusing to compromise on SDI development.
In 1986 Reagan denied that the selling of defensive weapons to Iran
for release of hostages held in Lebanon was part of an arms-for-
hostages deal, and the fallout from the Iran-Contra affair widened.

★ ★ ★

On my desk in the Oval Office, I have a little sign that says: There is no limit to what a man can do or where he can go if he doesn't mind who gets the credit.

—from White House Conference for a Drug Free America, February 29, 1988

Freedom is not the sole prerogative of a chosen few; it is the universal right of all God's children. Look to where peace and prosperity flourish today. It is in homes that freedom built. Victories against poverty are greatest and peace most secure where people live by laws that ensure free press, free speech, and freedom to worship, vote, and create wealth.

—from State of the Union Address, February 6, 1985

[O]ur work can never be truly done until every man, woman, and child shares in our gift, in our hope, and stands with us in the light of Liberty—the light that, tonight, will shortly cast its glow upon her, as it has upon us for two centuries, keeping faith with a dream of long ago and guiding millions still to a future of peace and freedom.

—from Statue of Liberty Centennial Celebration, New York, July 3, 1986

That system [government is the people's servant] has never failed us, but for a time we failed the system.

—from Second Presidential Inaugural Address, January 21, 1985

Once during the campaign, I said, "This is a wonderful time to be alive." And I meant that. I meant that we're lucky not to live in pale and timid times. We've been blessed with the opportunity to stand for something—for liberty and freedom and fairness. And these are things worth fighting for, worth devoting our lives to. And we have good reason to be hopeful and optimistic.

We've made much progress already. So, let us go forth with good cheer and stout hearts—happy warriors out to seize back a country and a world to freedom.

—from Annual Dinner of the Conservative Political
Action Conference, March 1, 1985

Today the United States Senate began a rendezvous with history. The threads of our past, present, and future as a nation will soon converge on the single overriding question before that body: Can we at last, after decades of drift, neglect, and excess, put our fiscal house in order? Can we assure a strong and prosperous future for ourselves, our children, and their children by adopting a plan that will compel the Federal Government to end the dangerous addiction to deficit spending and finally live within its means?

—from Address to the Nation, April 24, 1985

THE STORYTELLER

A fellow . . . was driving down a country road, and all of a sudden he looked out and there beside him was a chicken—he was doing about forty-five and the chicken was running alongside.

So he stepped on the gas, he got it up to about sixty, and the chicken caught up with him and was right beside him again, and then he thought, as he was looking at him, that the chicken had three legs. But before he could really make up his mind for sure, the chicken took off out in front of him at sixty miles an hour and turned down a lane into a barnyard.

Well, he made a quick turn and went down into the barnyard, too, and there was a farmer standing there, and he asked [the farmer], "Did a chicken come past you?" And [the farmer] said, "Yeah."

Well, [the driver] said, "Am I crazy or did the chicken have three legs?"

He says, "Yep, it's mine. . . . I breed three-legged chickens."

And the fellow said, "For heaven sakes, why?"

Well, [the farmer] says, "I like the drumstick, and Ma likes the drumstick, and now the kid likes the drumstick, and we just got tired of fighting for it."

And the driver said, "Well, how does it taste?"

He says, "I don't know. I've never been able to catch one."

—FROM FUND-RAISING DINNER FOR SENATOR MACK MATTINGLY,
ATLANTA, GEORGIA, JUNE 5, 1985

We in government should learn to look at our country through the eyes of the entrepreneur, seeing possibilities where others see only problems.

—from Radio Address to the Nation, January 26, 1985

We stand on the threshold of a great ability to produce more, do more, be more.

—from State of the Union Address,
February 6, 1985

If we can put a man on the moon, we can find ways to heat and light our homes and industries.

—from State of the State, January 9, 1974

To many of us now, computers, silicon chips, data processing, cybernetics, and all the other innovations of the dawning high-technology age are as mystifying as the workings of the combustion engine must have been when that first Model T rattled down Main Street, U.S.A. But as surely as America's pioneer spirit made us the industrial giant of the twentieth century, the same pioneer spirit today is opening up on another vast front of opportunity, the frontier of high technology.

—from State of the Union Address,
January 25, 1983

The explorers of the modern era are the entrepreneurs, men with vision, with the courage to take risks and faith enough to brave the unknown. These entrepreneurs and their small enterprises are responsible for almost all the economic growth in the United States. They are the prime movers of the technological revolution. In fact, one of the largest personal computer firms [Apple] in the United States was started by two college students, no older than you, in the garage behind their home. Some people, even in my own country, look at the riot of experiment that is the free market and see only waste. What of all the entrepreneurs that fail? Well, many do, particularly the successful ones; often several times. And if you ask them the secret of their success, they'll tell you it's all that they learned in their struggles along the way; yes, it's what they learned from failing. Like an athlete in competition or a scholar in pursuit of the truth, experience is the greatest teacher.

—from Q&A with the students and faculty at
Moscow State University, May 31, 1988

History is no captive of some inevitable force. History is made by men and women of vision and courage.

—from State of the Union Address,
February 4, 1986

★ ★ ★

THE GREAT COMMUNICATOR

A sparkling economy spurs initiatives, sunrise industries, and makes older ones more competitive.

Nowhere is this more important than our next frontier: space. Nowhere do we so effectively demonstrate our technological leadership and ability to make life better on Earth. The Space Age is barely a quarter of a century old. But already we've pushed civilization forward with our advances in science and technology. Opportunities and jobs will multiply as we cross new thresholds of knowledge and reach deeper into the unknown.

Our progress in space—taking giant steps for all mankind—is a tribute to American teamwork and excellence. Our finest minds in government, industry, and academia have all pulled together. And we can be proud to say: We are first; we are the best; and we are so because we're free.

America has always been greatest when we dared to be great. We can reach for greatness again. We can follow our dreams to distant stars, living and working in space for peaceful, economic, and scientific gain. . . . Just as the oceans opened up a new world for clipper ships and Yankee traders, space holds enormous potential for commerce today. The market for space transportation could surpass our capacity to develop it. . . . And as we develop the frontier of space, let us remember our responsibility to preserve our older resources here on Earth. Preservation of our environment is not a liberal or conservative challenge, it's common sense.

—FROM STATE OF THE UNION ADDRESS, JANUARY 25, 1984

I know it is hard to understand, but sometimes painful things like this happen. It's all part of the process of exploration and discovery. It's all part of taking a chance and expanding man's horizons. The future doesn't belong to the fainthearted; it belongs to the brave.

—from Address to the Nation on the loss of the space shuttle
Challenger, January 28, 1986

President Reagan and his staff watching a televised replay of the space shuttle Challenger *explosion in the Oval Office study. From left to right: Larry Speakes, Dennis Thomas, Jim Kuhn, President Reagan, Pat Buchanan, Don Regan, January 28, 1986.*

Did You Know? ★ On January 28, 1986, seventy-three seconds after liftoff from the Kennedy Space Center at Cape Canaveral, Florida, the space shuttle *Challenger* broke apart and disintegrated, taking the lives of seven crew members, including Christa McAuliffe, who was to be the first teacher in space. She had taught high school social studies in New Hampshire and was planning to teach on live television and in filmed lessons while in space. In 2004 the *Challenger* crew was awarded the Congressional Space Medal of Honor.

We will never forget them, nor the last time we saw them this morning, as they prepared for their journey and waved good-bye and "slipped the surly bonds of earth" to "touch the face of God."

— from Address to the Nation on the loss of the space shuttle
Challenger, January 28, 1986

We paused together to mourn and honor the valor of our seven *Challenger* heroes. And I hope that we are now ready to do what they would want us to do: Go forward, America, and reach for the stars. We will never forget those brave seven, but we shall go forward.

— from State of the Union Address, February 4, 1986

For all the stress and strain of recent ordeals, the United States is still a young nation, a nation that draws renewed strength not only from its material abundance and economic might but from free ideals that are as vibrant today as they were more than two centuries ago when that small but gallant band we call our Founding Fathers pledged their lives, their fortunes, and their sacred honor to win freedom and independence.

My fellow legionnaires, the American dream lives — not only in the hearts and minds of our own countrymen but in the hearts and minds of millions of the world's people in both free and oppressed societies who look to us for leadership. As long as that dream lives, as long as we continue to defend it, America has a future, and all mankind has reason to hope.

—from Annual Washington Conference of the American Legion,
February 22, 1983

Anything is possible in America if we have the faith, the will, and the heart. History is asking us once again to be a force for good in the world. Let us begin in unity, with justice, and love.

—from State of the Union Address, February 6, 1985

President Reagan presenting a Congressional Medal of Honor to the Vietnam Unknown Soldier during a Memorial Day ceremony at Arlington National Cemetery in Virginia, May 28, 1984.

As I flew back this evening, I had many thoughts. In just
a few days families across America will gather to celebrate
Thanksgiving. And again, as our forefathers who voyaged to
America, we traveled to Geneva with peace as our goal and
freedom as our guide. For there can be no greater good than
the quest for peace and no finer purpose than the preservation
of freedom. It is 350 years since the first Thanksgiving, when
Pilgrims and Indians huddled together on the edge of an
unknown continent. And now here we are gathered together on
the edge of an unknown future, but, like our forefathers, really not
so much afraid, but full of hope and trusting in God, as ever.
—from Address before Congress following the Soviet-U.S.
summit meeting in Geneva, November 21, 1985

We want to make this a more peaceful world. We want to reduce
arms. We want agreements that truly diminish the nuclear danger.
We don't just want signing ceremonies and color photographs of
leaders toasting each other with champagne. We want more.
We want real agreements, agreements that really work, with no
cheating. We want an end to state policies of intimidation, threats,
and the constant quest for domination. We want real peace.
—from Address to the Nation,
February 26, 1986

*President Reagan saying the Pledge of Allegiance during a visit
to St. Agatha's Catholic High School in Detroit, Michigan,
October 10, 1984.*

THE GREAT COMMUNICATOR

Now, for the benefit of these outlaw governments who are sponsoring international terrorism against our nation, I'm prepared to offer a brief lesson in American history. A number of times in America's past, foreign tyrants, warlords, and totalitarian dictators have misinterpreted the well-known likeability, patience, and generosity of the American people as signs of weakness or even decadence. Well, it's true; we are an easygoing people, slow to wrath, hesitant to see danger looming over every horizon. But it's also true that when the emotions of the American people are aroused, when their patriotism and their anger are triggered, there are no limits to their national valor nor their consuming passion to protect this nation's cherished tradition of freedom. . . .

Yes, we Americans have our disagreements, sometimes noisy ones, almost always in public—that's the nature of our open society—but no foreign power should mistake disagreement for disunity. Those who are tempted to do so should reflect on our national character and our history—a history littered with the wreckage of regimes who made the mistake of underestimating the vigor and will of the American people.

So, let me today speak for a united people. Let me say simply: We're Americans. We love this country. We love what she stands for, and we will always defend her. . . . We live for freedom—our own, our children's—and we will always stand ready to sacrifice for that freedom.

—FROM AMERICAN BAR ASSOCIATION, JULY 8, 1985, REFERRING TO THE HIJACKING OF TWA FLIGHT 847 ON JUNE 14 (ALL WERE EVENTUALLY FREED, EXCEPT FOR A NAVY DIVER WHO WAS BEATEN TO DEATH)

We Americans are slow to anger. We always seek peaceful avenues before resorting to the use of force—and we did. We tried quiet diplomacy, public condemnation, economic sanctions, and demonstrations of military force. None succeeded. Despite our repeated warnings, Qadhafi continued his reckless policy of intimidation, his relentless pursuit of terror. He counted on America to be passive. He counted wrong. I warned that there should be no place on Earth where terrorists can rest and train and practice their deadly skills. I meant it. I said that we would act with others, if possible, and alone if necessary to ensure that terrorists have no sanctuary anywhere. Tonight, we have.

—from Address to the Nation on the U.S. air strike against Libya in response to Libyan terrorist bombing (on April 5, 1986) of a West Berlin disco, injuring hundreds and killing two U.S. servicemen, April 14, 1986

[T]he grave threat of terrorism also jeopardizes the hopes for peace. No cause, no grievance, can justify it. Terrorism is heinous and intolerable. It is the crime of cowards—cowards who prey on the innocent, the defenseless, and the helpless.

—from 41st Session of the UN General Assembly, New York, September 22, 1986

[W]e Americans place far less weight upon the words that are spoken at meetings such as these than upon the deeds that follow. When it comes to human rights and judging Soviet intentions, we're all from Missouri—you got to show us.

—from Address to the Nation, October 13, 1986

Freedom is the right to question and change the established way of doing things. It is the continuing revolution of the marketplace. It is the understanding that allows us to recognize shortcomings and seek solutions. It is the right to put forth an idea, scoffed at by the experts, and watch it catch fire among the people. It is the right to dream—to follow your dream or stick to your conscience, even if you're the only one in a sea of doubters. Freedom is the recognition that no single person, no single authority or government has a monopoly on the truth, but that every individual life is infinitely precious, that every one of us put on this world has been put there for a reason and has something to offer.

—from Q&A with the students and faculty at
Moscow State University, May 31, 1988

*President Reagan at the recommissioning ceremony
for the battleship USS New Jersey,
Long Beach, California, December 28, 1982.*

President Reagan digging a trench at Rancho del Cielo, November 19, 1984.

Now, critics dubbed our plan Reaganomics and predicted economic ruin. Let's look at what's happened instead. Inflation has fallen from more than 12 percent to less than 9 percent. Interest rates are down. Mortgage rates are down and housing starts are up, helping industries like timber. And just listen to this: During these nearly four years of economic growth, we've seen the creation of more than 11 million jobs in the United States. Now, that is more jobs than Western Europe and Japan put together have created in the last ten years. You know, I could tell our economic program was working when they stopped calling it Reaganomics.

—from campaign rally for Senator Mack Mattingly,
Atlanta, Georgia, October 8, 1986

The history of these United States of America is indeed a history of individual achievement. It was their hard work that built our cities and farmed our prairies; their genius that continually pushed us beyond the boundaries of existing knowledge, reshaping our world with the steam engine, polio vaccine, and the silicon chip. It was their faith in freedom and love of country that sustained us through trials and hardships and through wars, and it was their courage and selflessness that enabled us to always prevail.

—from signing of the Tax Reform Act of 1986, October 22, 1986

President Reagan giving a speech at the Berlin Wall, Brandenburg Gate, Federal Republic of Germany, June 12, 1987.

9

Are You Better Off Than You Were Eight Years Ago?

SECOND TERM: 1987–1988

If anyone expects just a proud recitation of the accomplishments of my administration, I say let's leave that to history; we're not finished yet. So, my message to you tonight is put on your workshoes; we're still on the job.

—from State of the Union Address, January 25, 1988

IN 1987 THE TOWER COMMISSION CONCLUDED THAT REAGAN'S staff misled him about Iran-Contra and Reagan admitted that mistakes were made. The United States provided arms to both combatants in the Iran-Iraq war. In a famous speech at the Brandenburg Gate Reagan addresses Gorbachev directly with an imperative, "tear down this wall," referring to the Berlin Wall that had divided Germany into East Germany and West Germany since

1961. Almost two and a half years later, it would be torn down by Germans on both sides of the Berlin Wall and a reunited Germany would ensue. U.S.-Soviet relations greatly improved, largely due to the idealism and personal chemistry of the two leaders, and at the end of the year Reagan and Gorbachev signed a treaty to reduce their nuclear weapons by 4 percent, the first such arms' reduction agreement.

In 1988, Vice President George H. W. Bush—the Republican presidential nominee—defeated Michael Dukakis in the general election. Reagan gave his farewell address to the nation stressing that the Reagan Revolution had made a difference, and he left office with the highest approval rating of all the Presidents since FDR.

★ ★ ★

May I congratulate all of you who are Members of this historic 100th Congress of the United States of America. In this 200th anniversary year of our Constitution, you and I stand on the shoulders of giants—men whose words and deeds put wind in the sails of freedom. However, we must always remember that our Constitution is to be celebrated not for being old, but for being young—young with the same energy, spirit, and promise that filled each eventful day in Philadelphia's statehouse. We will be guided tonight by their acts, and we will be guided forever by their words.

—from State of the Union Address, January 27, 1987

President Reagan and Soviet General Secretary Gorbachev signing the INF Treaty in the East Room of the White House, December 8, 1987.

President Reagan working at his Oval Office desk on his first full day as President, January 21, 1981.

One of the things about the Presidency is that you're always somewhat apart. You spend a lot of time going by too fast in a car someone else is driving, and seeing the people through tinted glass—the parents holding up a child, and the wave you saw too late and couldn't return. And so many times I wanted to stop and reach out from behind the glass, and connect.

—from Farewell Address to the Nation, January 11, 1989

[This story is about] a man who became the chairman of his small-town charity. And, looking at the records, he went to a citizen of the town who had a six-figure income and who had never contributed to the town charity. And he called his attention to this fact and said that the record showed that, "You have this income that you've never contributed."

And [the citizen] said, "Do your records also show that my brother was wounded in the war, permanently disabled and never able to work again? Do they show that my sister was widowed with several children, and there was no insurance, there was no means of subsistence?"

And kind of abashed, the chairman said, "Well, no, the records don't show that."

"Well," he said, "I don't give anything to them; why should I give something to you?"

—from Awards Presentation Ceremony for the President's Committee on the Arts and the Humanities, May 17, 1983

What our citizens must know is this: America faces a disease that
is fatal and spreading. And this calls for urgency, not panic. It calls
for compassion, not blame. And it calls for understanding, not
ignorance. It's also important that America not reject those who
have the disease, but care for them with dignity and kindness.
Final judgment is up to God; our part is to ease the suffering
and to find a cure. This is a battle against disease, not against our
fellow Americans. We mustn't allow those with the AIDS virus to
suffer discrimination. . . . We must firmly oppose discrimination
against those who have AIDS. We must prevent the persecution,
through ignorance or malice, of our fellow citizens.
> —from speech to American Foundation for AIDS Research
> (amfAR), May 31, 1987

Did You Know? ★ AIDS was first identified in 1981. By
the time Reagan made his May 31, 1987, amfAR speech,
the epidemic had already claimed the lives of over twenty
thousand Americans, including the Reagans' close friend
actor Rock Hudson.

Now, what should happen when you make a mistake is this: You
take your knocks, you learn your lessons, and then you move on.
> —from Address to the Nation on the Iran-Contra scandal,
> March 4, 1987

President Reagan receiving the Tower Commission Report in the Cabinet Room with John Tower, January 26, 1987.

How am I supposed to get anyplace with the Russians if they keep dying on me?

—*The New York Times,* November 18, 1990, on the death of three Soviet Premiers—Leonid Brezhnev (1982), Yuri Andropov (1984), and Konstantin Chernenko (1985)— before Gorbachev became Premier in 1985

I recently heard a statement by an eminent scholar in our land who visited the Soviet Union recently. He is fluent in the Russian language. But on his way to the airport here, he recognized the youth of the cabdriver and got into conversation, found out he was working his way through college, and he asked him what he intended to be. And the young man said, "I haven't decided yet." Well, by coincidence, when he got to the Soviet Union and got in a cab, he had an equally young cabdriver. And speaking Russian, he got in conversation with him and asked the same question, finally, about the young man, what did he intend to be? And the young man said, "They haven't told me yet."

—from announcing America's Economic Bill of Rights, July 3, 1987

The West won't contain communism, it will transcend communism.

—from commencement exercises at the University of Notre Dame, May 17, 1981

★★★

THE GREAT COMMUNICATOR

The common interests have to do with the things of everyday life for people everywhere. Just suppose with me for a moment that an Ivan and an Anya could find themselves, oh, say, in a waiting room, or sharing a shelter from the rain or a storm with a Jim and Sally, and there was no language barrier to keep them from getting acquainted. Would they then debate the differences between their respective governments? Or would they find themselves comparing notes about their children and what each other did for a living?

Before they parted company, they would probably have touched on ambitions and hobbies and what they wanted for their children and problems of making ends meet. And as they went their separate ways, maybe Anya would be saying to Ivan, "Wasn't she nice? She also teaches music." Or Jim would be telling Sally what Ivan did or didn't like about his boss. They might even have decided they were all going to get together for dinner some evening soon. Above all, they would have proven that people don't make wars.

People want to raise their children in a world without fear and without war. They want to have some of the good things over and above bare subsistence that make life worth living. They want to work at some craft, trade, or profession that gives them satisfaction and a sense of worth. Their common interests cross all borders.

—FROM ADDRESS TO THE NATION,
JANUARY 16, 1984

The strength of the Solidarity movement in Poland demonstrates the truth told in an underground joke in the Soviet Union. It is that the Soviet Union would remain a one-party nation even if an opposition party were permitted, because everyone would join the opposition party.

—from Westminster speech delivered to the
British House of Commons, June 4, 1982

A nuclear war cannot be won, and must never be fought.
—from State of the Union Address,
January 25, 1984

My fellow Americans, I'm pleased to tell you today that I've signed legislation that will outlaw Russia forever. We begin bombing in five minutes.

—Reagan made this joking sound check before a speech
that did not go on air, August 11, 1984

[W]e do not mistrust each other because we are armed; we are armed because we mistrust each other.

—from World Affairs Council of Massachusetts,
Springfield, Massachusetts, April 21, 1988

General Secretary Gorbachev, if you seek peace, if you seek
prosperity for the Soviet Union and Eastern Europe, if you seek
liberalization: Come here to this gate! Mr. Gorbachev, open this
gate! Mr. Gorbachev, tear down this wall!

—from remarks on East-West relations,
Brandenburg Gate in West Berlin, June 12, 1987

More than a century ago a young Frenchman, Alexis de
Tocqueville, visited America. After that visit he predicted that
the two great powers of the future world would be, on one hand,
the United States, which would be built, as he said, "by the
plowshare," and, on the other, Russia, which would go forward,
again, as he said, "by the sword." Yet need it be so? Cannot swords
be turned to plowshares? Can we and all nations not live in peace?
In our obsession with antagonisms of the moment, we often forget
how much unites all the members of humanity. Perhaps we need
some outside, universal threat to make us recognize this common
bond. I occasionally think how quickly our differences worldwide
would vanish if we were facing an alien threat from outside this
world. And yet, I ask you, is not an alien force already among
us? What could be more alien to the universal aspirations of our
peoples than war and the threat of war?

—from 42nd Session of the UN General Assembly,
New York, September 21, 1987

conclude in just telling you one of those jokes which illustrates the sense of humor. And this is the one that I told Gorbachev.

It seems that they recently issued an order that anyone that's caught speeding must get a ticket. And you know that most of the driving there is done by the Politburo, by the—or the bureaucracy. They're the ones with cars and drivers and so forth. So, it seems that one morning Gorbachev himself came out of his country home, knew he was late getting to the Kremlin, told his driver to get in the back seat, and he'd drive. And down the road he went, past two motorcycle policemen. One of them took out after him. In a few minutes, he's back with his buddy, and the buddy said, "Did you give him a ticket?"

He said, "No."

"Well," [the buddy] said, "why not? We were told that anyone caught speeding was to get a ticket."

He said, "No, no, this one was too important."

"Well," [the buddy] said, "who was it?"

He says, "I don't know. I couldn't recognize him, but his driver was Gorbachev."

—FROM WORLD AFFAIRS COUNCIL OF MASSACHUSETTS,
SPRINGFIELD, MASSACHUSETTS, APRIL 21, 1988

Yes, at every point on the map that the Soviets have applied pressure, we've done all we can to apply pressure against them. And now we're seeing a sight many believed they would never see in our lifetime: the receding of the tide of totalitarianism.

—from Georgetown University's
Bicentennial Convocation, October 1, 1988

America is a nation made up of hundreds of nationalities. Our ties to you are more than ones of good feeling; they're ties of kinship. In America, you'll find Russians, Armenians, Ukrainians, peoples from Eastern Europe and Central Asia. They come from every part of this vast continent, from every continent, to live in harmony, seeking a place where each cultural heritage is respected, each is valued for its diverse strengths and beauties and the richness it brings to our lives.

—from Q&A with the students and faculty
at Moscow State University, May 31, 1988

[W]hen we look back at the time of choosing, we can say that we did all that could be done—never less.

—from Republican National Convention,
New Orleans, Louisiana, August 15, 1988

America is committed to the world because so much of the world
is inside America. After all, only a few miles from this very room
is our Statue of Liberty, past which life began anew for millions,
where the peoples from nearly every country in this hall joined
to build these United States. The blood of each nation courses
through the American vein and feeds the spirit that compels us to
involve ourselves in the fate of this good Earth.

—from 40th Session of UN General Assembly,
New York, October 24, 1985

So, let us remember the children and the future we want for
them. And let us never forget that this promise of peace and
freedom, the gift that is ours as Americans, the gift that we seek to
share with all the world, depends for its strength on the spiritual
source from which it comes. So, during this holy season, let us
also reflect that in the prayers of simple people there is more
power and might than that possessed by all the great statesmen or
armies of the Earth.

—from Address to the Nation, December 10, 1987

*President Reagan (with Nancy) giving a speech on the Centennial
of the Statue of Liberty, Governor's Island, New York, July 4, 1986.*

The Reagans visiting the grave of Theodore Roosevelt Jr. during a trip to Normandy, France, for the fortieth anniversary of D-Day, June 6, 1984.

And our own experience on this continent—the American experience—though brief, has had one unmistakable encounter, an insistence on the preservation of one sacred truth. It is a truth that our first President, our Founding Father, passed on in the first farewell address made to the American people. It is a truth that I hope now you'll permit me to mention in these remarks of farewell, a truth embodied in our Declaration of Independence: that the case for inalienable rights, that the idea of human dignity, that the notion of conscience above compulsion can be made only in the context of higher law, only in the context of what one of the founders of this organization, Secretary-General Dag Hammarskjold, has called devotion to something which is greater and higher than we are ourselves. This is the endless cycle, the final truth to which humankind seems always to return: that religion and morality, that faith in something higher, are prerequisites for freedom and that justice and peace within ourselves is the first step toward justice and peace in the world and for the ages.

 —from 43rd Session of the UN General Assembly, New York, September 26, 1988

When we finish this luncheon, I hope you'll stick around a little while. We're having a tag sale upstairs, and everything must go.

 —from Presentation Ceremony for the Presidential Medal of Freedom, January 19, 1989

THE GREAT COMMUNICATOR

The past few days . . . I've thought a bit of the "shining city upon a hill." The phrase comes from John Winthrop, who wrote it to describe the America he imagined. What he imagined was important because he was an early Pilgrim, an early freedom man. He journeyed here on what today we'd call a little wooden boat; and like the other Pilgrims, he was looking for a home that would be free.

I've spoken of the shining city all my political life, but I don't know if I ever quite communicated what I saw when I said it. But in my mind it was a tall, proud city built on rocks stronger than oceans, wind-swept, God-blessed, and teeming with people of all kinds living in harmony and peace; a city with free ports that hummed with commerce and creativity. And if there had to be city walls, the walls had doors and the doors were open to anyone with the will and the heart to get here. That's how I saw it, and see it still.

And how stands the city on this winter night? More prosperous, more secure, and happier than it was eight years ago. But more than that: After two hundred years, two centuries, she still stands strong and true on the granite ridge, and her glow has held steady no matter what storm. And she's still a beacon, still a magnet for all who must have freedom, for all the pilgrims from all the lost places who are hurtling through the darkness, toward home. . . .

We did it. We weren't just marking time. We made a difference. We made the city stronger, we made the city freer, and we left her in good hands. All in all, not bad; not bad at all.

—FROM FAREWELL ADDRESS TO THE NATION, JANUARY 11, 1989

But, you know, I'll rest a whole lot easier knowing that I've left the White House in good hands. There hasn't been a transition like this since Inauguration Day in 1837, when Andrew Jackson turned the keys to the store over to Martin Van Buren. And, no, I don't remember that day. When you get to be my age, you don't remember anything that recent.

—from remarks to administration officials on Domestic Policy, December 13, 1988

Did You Know? ★ Reagan often referenced Puritan John Winthrop's 1630 sermon "A Model of Christian Charity" in his speeches. Winthrop's ideal of a "shining city upon a hill"—an image that invokes the promise of America and American exceptionalism—has also been used by other Presidents, such as John F. Kennedy.

And while our feet have been planted on the ground, our eyes have been turned toward the stars.

—from remarks to administration officials on Domestic Policy, December 13, 1988

*President Reagan leaving the Oval Office for the last time,
January 20, 1989.*

10

Sunset Years

America's best days are yet to come. Our proudest
moments are yet to be. Our most glorious
achievements are just ahead.

—from Republican National Convention,
Houston, Texas, August 17, 1992

Reagan's anticommunist hard line and the weakened Soviet economy led to the fall of the Berlin Wall in November 1989 and to the dissolution of the Soviet Union and the end of the Cold War in December 1991.

In 1994 Reagan made public to the nation that he had Alzheimer's disease to promote greater awareness and understanding of the disease.

In 1996, Reagan's brother, Neil, died of heart failure at the age of eighty-eight.

In 2001, Reagan's oldest daughter, Maureen, died of cancer at the age of sixty. Unfortunately, he was unable to attend her funeral.

Ronald Wilson Reagan died of pneumonia on June 5, 2004, at the age of ninety-three.

★ ★ ★

Contrary to some of the things you've heard, I'm the same man I was when I came to Washington. I believe the same things I believed when I came to Washington. And I think those beliefs have been vindicated by the success of the policies to which we held fast.

—from Georgetown University's Bicentennial Convocation, October 1, 1988

And . . . I won a nickname, "The Great Communicator." But I never thought it was my style or the words I used that made a difference: it was the content. I wasn't a great communicator, but I communicated great things, and they didn't spring full bloom from my brow, they came from the heart of a great nation—from our experience, our wisdom, and our belief in the principles that have guided us for two centuries. They called it the Reagan revolution. Well, I'll accept that, but for me it always seemed more like the great rediscovery, a rediscovery of our values and our common sense.

—from Farewell Address to the Nation, January 11, 1989

President Reagan's last day saluting as he boards Marine One *at the U.S. Capitol, January 20, 1989.*

The Reagans at the 1988 Republican National Convention at the Superdome in New Orleans, Louisiana, August 15, 1988.

★ ★ ★

THE GREAT COMMUNICATOR

When our children turn the pages of our lives, I hope they'll see that we had a vision to pass forward a nation as nearly perfect as we could, where there's decency, tolerance, generosity, honesty, courage, common sense, fairness, and piety. This is my vision, and I'm grateful to God for blessing me with a good life and a long one. But when I pack up my bags in Washington, don't expect me to be happy to hear all this talk about the twilight of my life.

Twilight? Twilight? Not in America. Here, it's a sunrise every day—fresh new opportunities, dreams to build. Twilight? That's not possible, because I confess there are times when I feel like I'm still little Dutch Reagan racing my brother down the hill to the swimming hole under the railroad bridge over the Rock River. You see, there's no sweeter day than each new one, because here in our country it means something wonderful can happen to you. And something wonderful happened to me.

We lit a prairie fire a few years back. Those flames were fed by passionate ideas and convictions, and we were determined to make them run all—burn, I should say, all across America. And what times we've had! Together we've fought for causes we love. But we can never let the fire go out or quit the fight, because the battle is never over. Our freedom must be defended over and over again—and then again.

— FROM REPUBLICAN NATIONAL CONVENTION,
NEW ORLEANS, LOUISIANA, AUGUST 15, 1988

[B]ecause we're a great nation, our challenges seem complex. It will always be this way. But as long as we remember our first principles and believe in ourselves, the future will always be ours. And something else we learned: Once you begin a great movement, there's no telling where it will end. We meant to change a nation, and instead, we changed a world.

—from Farewell Address to the Nation,

January 11, 1989

We sometimes forget that even those who came here first to settle the new land were also strangers. I've spoken before of the tiny *Arabella*, a ship at anchor just off the Massachusetts coast. A little group of Puritans huddled on the deck.

And then John Winthrop, who would later become the first Governor of Massachusetts, reminded his fellow Puritans there on that tiny deck that they must keep faith with their God, that the eyes of all the world were upon them, and that they must not forsake the mission that God had sent them on, and they must be a light unto the nations of all the world—a shining city upon a hill.

—from Statue of Liberty Centennial Celebration,

New York, July 3, 1986

My fondest hope is that Americans will travel the road extending forward from the arch of experience, never forgetting our heroic origins, never failing to seek divine guidance as we march boldly, bravely into a future limited only by our capacity to dream.

—from the opening of the Ronald Reagan Presidential Foundation and Library, Simi Valley, California, November 4, 1991

Did You Know? ★ The Ronald Reagan Presidential Foundation and Library is a federally operated presidential library located in Simi Valley, California, forty miles from Los Angeles, and its street address is 40 Presidential Drive, honoring Reagan as the nation's fortieth President. When it was dedicated in 1991, five former and current Presidents attended, including Reagan, and beyond serving as the repository for Reagan's presidential papers and documents it is also where he was interred.

Emerson was right; we are the country of tomorrow. Our revolution did not end at Yorktown. More than two centuries later, America remains on a voyage of discovery, a land that has never become, but is always in the act of becoming.

—from Republican National Convention, Houston, Texas, August 17, 1992

My Fellow Americans,

I have recently been told that I am one of the millions of Americans who will be afflicted with Alzheimer's Disease.

Upon learning this news, Nancy & I had to decide whether as private citizens we would keep this a private matter or whether we would make this news known in a public way.

In the past Nancy suffered from breast cancer and I had my cancer surgeries. We found through our open disclosures we were able to raise public awareness. We were happy that as a result many more people underwent testing. They were treated in early stages and able to return to normal, healthy lives.

So now, we feel it is important to share it with you. In opening our hearts, we hope this might promote greater awareness of this condition. Perhaps it will encourage a clearer understanding of the individuals and families who are affected by it.

At the moment I feel just fine. I intend to live the remainder of the years God gives me on this earth doing the things I have always done. I will continue to share life's journey with my beloved Nancy and my family. I plan to enjoy the great outdoors and stay in touch with my friends and supporters.

Unfortunately, as Alzheimer's Disease progresses, the family often bears a heavy burden. I only wish there was some way I could spare Nancy from this painful experience. When the time comes I am confident that with your help she will face it with faith and courage.

In closing let me thank you, the American people for giving me the great honor of allowing me to serve as your President. When the Lord calls me home, whenever that may be, I will leave with the greatest love for this country of ours and eternal optimism for its future.

I now begin the journey that will lead me into the sunset of my life. I know that for America there will always be a bright dawn ahead.

Thank you my friends. May God always bless you.

Sincerely,

Ronald Reagan

—text of handwritten letter to the American people,
November 5, 1994

Index

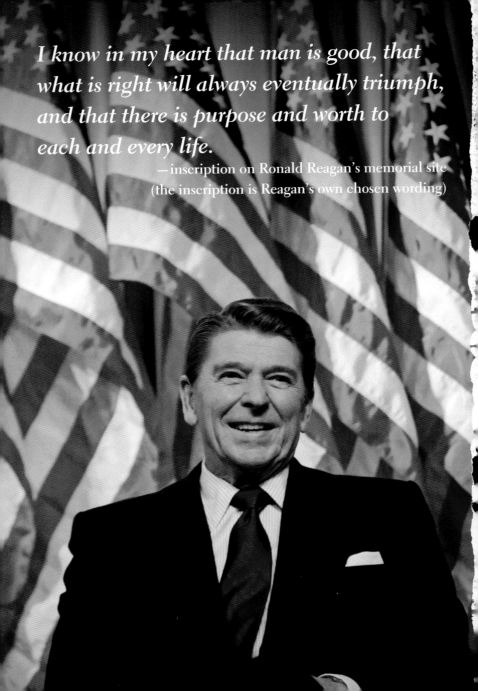

I know in my heart that man is good, that what is right will always eventually triumph, and that there is purpose and worth to each and every life.

—inscription on Ronald Reagan's memorial site
(the inscription is Reagan's own chosen wording)